Light and Variable

Praise for Connie Cronley

"Where Connie Cronley lives . . . is a wonderful place to visit, and return to, again and again, full of quiet magic and a calm that's capable of coming through any storm."
—Donald Westlake, author of the Dortmunder Novels

"[Cronley's] pieces sing with sharp humor and poke fun at the author's sharp foibles. . . . An adventurer at heart, Cronley also takes readers along on her journeys of discovery." —*Publishers Weekly*

"Connie Cronley is an essayist of unmatched skill. Her essays are unusual, arresting, and thought-provoking."
—Carolyn Hart, author of the Death on Demand
mystery series and *Letter from Home*

"Although her landscape is largely Oklahoma, Cronley transcends the open spaces and tall grasses to include a vision of the entire world. She is a writer of great charm, wit, and humanity."
—Edward Swift, author of *My Grandfather's Finger*
and *A Place with Promise*

"Cronley has a great gift for mixing hope and irony."
—Rennard Strickland, author of *Fire and the Spirits:
Cherokee Law from Clan to Court* and *Tonto's Revenge*

"Connie has the unique ability to tweak a feeling or memory we thought to have cleverly hidden. When she writes in all simplicity, it comes out deep and dear and so touching that I want more of it."
—Joyce Sequichie Hifler, author of *A Cherokee Feast of Days*

"Cronley . . . is a modern-day Mark Twain. She offers witty commentaries on the human condition, insightful observation on life's various vexations, and her sharp eye for the ridiculous and nostalgic will bring a rumble of laughter or a shimmering tear of recognition." —*Tulsa World*

Light and Variable

**A Year of Celebrations, Holidays,
Recipes, and Emily Dickinson**

*For David & Becky —
Thanks for all*

Connie Cronley

*you do for
Trinity and Iron
Gate.*

connie cronley

UNIVERSITY OF OKLAHOMA PRESS : NORMAN

21 Sept 2006

ALSO BY CONNIE CRONLEY

Sometimes a Wheel Falls Off (Tulsa, 1999)

Library of Congress Cataloging-in-Publication Data

Cronley, Connie
  Light and variable : a year of celebrations, holidays, recipes, and Emily
  Dickinson / Connie Cronley.
      p. cm.
  A collection of the author's public radio commentaries and freelance
  newspaper and magazine articles.
  ISBN 0-8061-3788-6 (alk. paper)
    I. Title

  PN4874.C85A25 2006
  814'.6—dc22   2006040389

Much of the material in this book appeared earlier as commentaries on public radio (KWGS 89.5 FM), in columns in *Tulsa People* magazine, or as articles in the *Tulsa World* newspaper and *Tulsa* magazine.

The poem "Casabianca" is from *The Complete Poems 1927–1979*, by Elizabeth Bishop, copyright ©1979, 1983 by Alice Helen Methfessel, reprinted in this volume by permission of Farrar, Straus, and Giroux, LLC. The poem "Poem about Heartbreak That Go On and On," by June Jordan, is copyright ©2005 June M Jordan Literary Estate Trust, reprinted in this volume by permission of the June M Jordan Literary Estate Trust, *www.junejordan.com*.

1   2   3   4   5   6   7   8   9   10

For

Nicolas and Harry
Dahvid and Maksim

Contents

March

April

May

Preface

I will tell you a story that will make you happy.

My book of essays from public radio, *Sometimes a Wheel Falls Off,* was dedicated to my cat Phoebe, who taught me about life, and with appreciation to Phillip and Marty. Nobody asked me who Phillip and Marty are. I will tell you. They are my therapist and my gynecologist, who helped me put the wheels back on my life.

The *Publishers Weekly* review of that book said that I am an adventurer at heart. Funny, I think of myself as a country mouse, but a mouse who took a while to understand that.

I grew up in a dinky town in northeastern Oklahoma, and I could not wait for the day I would find my true geography—Paris, perhaps, or Greenwich Village. Then I read Willa Cather and her love songs to the Great Plains. When she described the grass as a great buffalo hide and underneath the earth was galloping, galloping, galloping . . . I recognized my home. I saw the energy, strength, sorrow, and pride of it. Suddenly I knew that I am a prairie girl and that the expanse of Oklahoma prairies is the landscape of my heart.

"The time came when I began to ponder the mystery of my own background," said V. S. Naipaul in an interview in the *New York Times.* I understand that. There is no ordinary life or commonplace homeland.

The geography of my home state settled on me comfortably, like a well-balanced backpack, and I set off on the journey that was to be my life. Wind is a force to be reckoned with in Oklahoma. We are the nation's eighth-windiest state. The wind generates energy and wreaks destruction. The ceaseless wind drove some of the lonely pioneer women mad. The fierce winds whipped topsoil into black clouds during the Dust Bowl. I rail at the wind, respect the wind, and relish the wind, but I am happiest in the middle ground—with winds that are light and variable.

When I was a little girl, between my grandmother's strawberry patch and her kitchen door, hollyhocks towered over me. Now I grow hollyhocks myself, just outside the back door. They illustrate death and resurrection, said Father Stephen McKee, an Episcopal priest. I see them as a constant cycle of life in pastel colors.

The best time to plant the black, flat hollyhock seeds, I read, is in the winter. Sprinkle them on top of the snow and they will sink into the ground as the snow melts and germinate in the spring.

Those instructions must be for another climate. We do not have that much snow in Oklahoma. I plant hollyhock seeds in the fall or hollyhock plants in the spring, but I am more of a dabbler than a gardener. Year after year, my neighbor, an old country boy, will watch me plant things in the wrong time and at the wrong place and struggle along. I have a lot of surprises and many failures, but I never give up. "Having another crack at it, are you?" he says to me.

If the weather is not too wet or too cool, the hollyhocks grow and blossom in their second year. I prefer the old-fashioned, single-blossom hollyhocks in all colors with throats of another hue. Until tornado season, when the winds knock the hollyhocks askew, like Saturday night cowboys outside a dance hall, I walk through a stand of peach, violet, yellow, burgundy, and cream hollyhocks.

By late July, the broad leaves have been eaten to lace. "You could spray those," someone told me. "Get rid of the worms." I don't want to spray them. I just plant more hollyhocks to share with the green caterpillars. In the fall, the caterpillars turn into painted lady butterflies.

That is how we all are. If we can step into change, we are caterpillars becoming moths and butterflies. If we do not fly, we find our way as if crossing a stream, gingerly testing the stepping-stones. Sometimes we plunge ahead, stumble, and splash; sometimes we crawl; but we make it safely to shore.

Here is what I like to take on the journey:

- A sense of humor
- A big measure of joy
- A lot of gratitude
- Some tenacity. We do not always live on Easy Street, because sometimes life is hard. Move on, I remind myself. "Keep your eyes on the prize," as Martin Luther King, Jr., said. Don't settle down on Crybaby Ranch.
- A lot of common sense. This means we ought to take care of ourselves on the adventure. Try to remember to nurture our whole selves—emotionally, physically, and mentally. It should not be a chore. That is why enjoying a good stretch of the legs

and the art of the table is good. As my daddy used to say, "You've got to eat good food if you're going to have good fur on your back, belly, and sides."

- A foundation of spirituality. Almost any kind will do.
- Personal items. For me, that is Emily Dickinson—not the poems with the polite commas, but those with the breathless dashes and inventive capitalizations. A few heroes to admire and to learn from. Friends and family. Pets, however rascally they are. A love of nature.
- A funny look at time and place. I enjoy the eccentricities of our culture, our language, our celebrities. This is the world we live in.
- A reminder to celebrate life. This is why the essays in this book are loosely structured around a calendar year with both traditional and whimsical holidays.

Oh, I have my setbacks. My lucky bamboo died. I had a beauty accident and burned a red stripe across my forehead with the curling iron. Everybody recognized it for what it was and laughed at me. I caught my toe in the vacuum cleaner and oh my, the carrying on. But I press on.

And before I know it, I look past the bedraggled plants and lo! the hollyhocks have taken wing.

Acknowledgments

Seeing a book into print is much like making a chain of colored paper. Many people contribute to the process. I acknowledge with profound gratitude the following people who helped make this book possible. Many thanks to the staff of the University of Oklahoma Press, especially John Drayton and Kirk Bjornsgaard, but also Alice Stanton, DiAnne Huff, and Emmy Ezell, and freelance copy editor Sally Bennett. They are all consummate professionals and a joy to work with. I would also like to extend my thanks to William Bernhardt, Brian Byrne, Teresa Finders, Rich Fisher, Joseph Kestner, Missy Kruse, Jim Langdon, Cathy Logan, Teresa Miller, Juley Roffers, Keith Skrzypczak, Larry Silvey, and Joe Worley.

The poems of Emily Dickinson that I quote are from my favorite version: *The Complete Poems of Emily Dickinson,* edited by Thomas H. Johnson (Boston: Little, Brown, 1960 [orig. pub. 1890]).

The poem "Casabianca" is from *The Complete Poems, 1927–1979* by Elizabeth Bishop. Copyright © 1979, 1983 by Alice Helen Methfessel. Reprinted by permission of Farrar, Straus and Giroux, LLC.

The poem "Poem about Heartbreak That Go On and On," by June M Jordan is copyright © 2005 by June M Jordan Literary Estate Trust. Reprinted by permission of the June M Jordan Literary Estate Trust, www.junejordan.com.

Light and Variable

January

Like Brooms of Steel
The Snow and Wind
Had swept the Winter Street—

—Emily Dickinson,
from poem 1252

January 3 Is Festival of Sleep Day

Saints and Sinners and Movie Stars, Right Here

One of the most miserable New Year's Eves I ever spent was huddled in bed under piles of covers and cats, listening to an ice storm scratch at the window and reading the assignment for book club. It was a novel about bleak people in frozen Newfoundland.

The more I read about their loveless, lonely lives, the colder I got. When I heard a pathetic, single whistle sound at midnight, I thought, "It can't get any worse than this."

But things change—perspectives and the weather alike. A recent New Year's Eve was so warm that I sat outside at twilight in shirtsleeves drinking salty dogs made with juice from my sister's grapefruit trees in Tucson. It was just me and my dreams and my yellow dog, Bingo, gnawing a bone noisily. I thought, "It doesn't get any better than this."

I used to love going to glittery New Year's parties. One year I wore pink rosebuds in my hair. The last few years, I have loved spending the holiday alone. An ideal evening is warm socks, a chilly glass of champagne, and a new book I got for Christmas.

My friend Glenda makes it a practice every New Year's Day to read over her journal of the past year and to see what progress she has made. Oh Lord. It was tough enough getting through the year without having to revisit it.

What I read one recent New Year's Day was the *New York Times Magazine,* devoted to profiles of people who had died the previous year. I read about Marlon Brando, Ray Charles, Katharina Dalton (the physician who first wrote about PMS), Washington reporter Mary McGrory, Elisabeth Kubler-Ross (who wrote about death and dying), oilwell firefighter Red Adair, and Joe Gold of Gold's Gym. Some of the writers—

writers being what they are—wrote as much about themselves as they did the person who had died.

And then I came to Anthony Giardina's story about Tony Randall. This actor made his name, the article tells us, in romantic comedy movies of the 1950s and 1960s usually starring Doris Day and Rock Hudson. Tony Randall was their counterbalance, and what he embodied, the writer tells us, is "neurotic grandeur." Even glee.

A decade later, romantic comedies featured Jewish sad sacks Elliott Gould, George Segal, and Woody Allen, but the first one was Tony Randall, born Leonard Rosenberg in—and this is a quote from the article—"of all unlikely places, Tulsa, Oklahoma."

That's us—Tulsa of All Unlikely Places, Oklahoma. Big, corn-fed grins on our faces. Simple as pie. Happy as the day is long.

It has been suggested (and what's worse, suggested in all seriousness) that the City of Tulsa erect a statue to native son Tony Randall. Not that cities do not have statues of actors. Chicago has a statue of Bob Newhart; Raleigh, North Carolina, has statues of Andy Taylor and Ron Howard; New York has Jackie Gleason; Minneapolis has Mary Tyler Moore.

In fact, Tulsa has a statue honoring an actress, too. Jennifer Jones was Tulsa native Phylis Isley (born March 2, 1919) before she became a movie star. Her parents owned a touring tent show and later some movie theaters.

Phyl, as she was known, attended Monte Cassino Catholic school, spent a year at Northwestern University in Evanston, Illinois, and then went to the American Academy of Dramatic Arts in New York. There she met the young actor Robert Walker and brought him to Tulsa to perform with her in a weekly dramatic radio show. In 1939, they were married at Christ the King Catholic Church. She wore a red suit.

In Hollywood, as Phylis Walker, she appeared in B-movies: a western with John Wayne and a Dick Tracy serial. Her big break was the title role in the 1943 movie *Song of Bernadette*. She won an Academy Award for her portrayal of the French peasant girl whose visions transformed Lourdes into a place of miracles.

When the movie opened, Jones and her two young sons rode the train to Tulsa for a great homecoming. She wore a yellow-and-brown tweed suit and alligator pumps. To the surprise of her former schoolmates, she had a large felt hat. "Gone Hollywood," we would say today. Also, her name had been changed to Jennifer Jones.

"Welcome Home" banners were strung across downtown Tulsa streets, giant copies of Norman Rockwell's portrait of her were displayed in bank and department store windows, and her name blazed in lights at Fourth and Main, called "Tulsa's 'Little Times Square.'" It was all reported by *Photoplay* magazine. A statue as Bernadette was erected to her at Monte Cassino. She was twenty-five.

The press described her as a wholesome and beautiful young star who wore low heels ("low for Hollywood, at least"), slept nine or ten hours each night, drank a quart of milk a day, and did not smoke. She was an expert swimmer and a good tennis player. She devoted her spare time to the war effort.

Her next movie changed that reputation. In *Duel in the Sun*, she played a hot-blooded, half-breed wench lusting after Gregory Peck. Off screen, Jones was divorced and involved in an affair with married David O. Selznick, who later divorced his wife to marry her. Oh, the scandal of it all—but society's measure of scandal was different then.

The statue was taken down. When I asked the school officials about this, I was told that the statue had never been moved, but I heard this story from a university professor who was there.

Some sixty years have passed. The statue is back on the grounds of Monte Cassino. I checked—it's a peasant girl kneeling in prayer, although it does not look much like Jennifer Jones to me.

If we had a statue of gleefully neurotic Tony Randall, I wonder where we would put it. Would the temples compete for it, since he was Jewish? Should it go along the Arkansas River's bike and jogging path among the statues of the bison and eagles? Downtown by the Performing Arts Center, facing the statue of the Indian Ballerina? It is one of those great questions of life—where does fine art fit into contemporary society?

For fifteen years I was manager of Tulsa Ballet Theatre. While I was on an airplane going to a ballet conference in New York, the man sitting beside me looked at the materials I was reading and said, "Classical ballet in Oklahoma. What will they think of next?"

I wish I had thought to say, "I'll have you know, sir, that Leonard Rosenberg was from Tulsa, Oklahoma."

Does the rest of the country think we do not have culture? Or neurotics?

Why, we have people—right here in Tulsa (another irksome phrase) —who could be the subject of novels and petit scandals. If we were to write our own year-end magazine of local citizens who have died recently, I could write about the colorful, eccentric patron of the arts who wore a cape, carried a walking stick, and lived his last years in, we thought, genteel poverty, cadging free tickets to the ballet and opera. When he died, however, he was discovered to be a millionaire, and he had made his million selling soft porn—nude photos of Tulsa men to European audiences. His basement was full of boxes of the photographs.

Who among us, one might ask quietly, are those men? In fact, some of us did ask, but those who know would never tell, because this is, after all, Tulsa of All Places. We are a polite people who generally keep our neuroses tucked away and our private lives politely private.

On the other hand. I *always* eat black-eyed peas on New Year's Day, but this year when my cupboard was bare, I grew madcap and reckless and ate garbanzo beans instead.

You think that is not daring and brash? A person like that might do anything. Might even write year-end stories about Tulsans of All People.

My book club sisters said the book about Newfoundland changed their lives. It did not change my life, because I did not finish it. That is one thing I have already changed about my life: I no longer feel compelled to finish a book. I have soldiered on through too many books I did not like. No more. I give myself the courage to stop reading. A small step for literature, a giant step for self-empowerment. I am now working on applying the same theory to projects and people. If it drags me down, dump it. Move on briskly and keep up with my own life.

I have not yet perfected this, but I am practicing it much the same way the boy next door practices shooting baskets.

By January, I have come to terms with the short days and the cold that keeps me inside. My favorite January holiday is the Festival of Sleep Day, January 3. I must be part hedgehog or hamster, because hibernating comes easily to me these long nights. God knows I have already added extra body fat to sustain me through long sleep. I could sleep until April with this new girth. Luckily I read the tip about using a rubber band around my waistband button. Without it, my pants are so tight, if the button popped it would put out someone's eye.

After the holidays, I am satiated with social festivities and froufrou. I am more than ready to reclaim a life that is stark, clean, and simple. I appreciate the soberness of an Emily Dickinson winter:

Winter is good . . .
To Intellects inebriate
With Summer, or the World—

My body and mind are both inebriated with the world and with the
bottle of champagne I opened to have with a supper of scalloped oysters. Time to get into shape. Again. Move on, move on.

New Year's Eve Scalloped Oysters

2 cans oysters (do not drain)
½ cup (or more) light cream
3 cups (or so) cracker crumbs
½ cup butter, melted
¼ teaspoon pepper
Paprika

Heat oven to 375 degrees. Grease baking dish (11½" × 7") by melting butter in it. Put oysters and oyster liquor in baking dish; pour
about half the cream over oysters. Combine cracker crumbs, butter,
and pepper. Sprinkle cracker mixture over oysters. Pour remaining
cream over this. Don't let the whole mixture be too soggy; liquid
should come up about ¾ of the way. Sprinkle with paprika and
bake uncovered 30 to 40 minutes.
Serves four

A tart little salad is a nice accompaniment. Drink lots of very cold
champagne with this.

January 9 Is Play God Day

American Indian Times

I had an epiphany while vacuuming the other day. I do some of my best thinking when I am vacuuming. It is one of the unexpected benefits of having a houseful of cats.

Let me start at the beginning. I had been having trouble with a cranky neighbor, and negative vibes were coming my way over my white picket fence.

Then, when I was vacuuming I suddenly thought of my friend Janice and her spider bite. Janice is American Indian—Choctaw, Sac and Fox—and she has a master's degree in sociology, so she lives in two cultures. When she was giving me some background information for an article I was writing about urban Native Americans, she illustrated the difficulty of straddling these two worlds.

"I got a spider bite the other day," Janice said. "What's the first thing you would do if you got a spider bite?"

I gave her that blank look I have perfected over the years, so she went on without me. "You'd put medicine on it, right? That's what I did. I went to the medicine cabinet. But it didn't help. So I talked to my grandmother and she said, 'Did you try tobacco?' Now I knew that— it's an Indian remedy," Janice said, "but I forgot it. Forgot my Indian heritage for a minute."

Remembering that story made me think—smudge stick! That's what I need, a cedar-and-sage smudge stick to cleanse my house of the negative vibes coming from the neighbor. So I went to the Indian art store where I always get smudge sticks, but they were sold out.

"Oh no," I said. "I really need one. I'm trying to fight off some negative mojo."

The Indian man behind the counter did not bat an eye. "I know what you mean," he said. "I've had a lot of demand. It's the first of the year and everyone wants clean houses. I've got some sweet grass," he said.

"Oohh," I whined at the substitute. "It's better than nothing, but it's not the same thing."

"No," he said. "You need you some red cedar."

The reason I know about the healing powers of cedar—and tobacco—is not because of my interest in herbs, it is because of my Indian heritage. My Indian roots are tough, but then, they have to be, because all my life I have been tormented about my Cherokee blood by my cousin Carole Greenfeather.

She is half Shawnee, exotic looking with straight, dark hair, chiseled cheekbones, and eyes as black as an otter's. When I was a little girl and visited her in Wichita, she would threaten me, "If we meet any of my Indian friends and they ask you if you're Indian, you say no."

"But I am Indian," I would say. "I'm part Cherokee."

"Phew," she said scornfully. "Everybody is part Cherokee." Almost everybody around here is part Cherokee. She is, too, but she never claimed it.

One of my earliest memories was when she and I were about five years old at a stomp dance near White Oak in northeastern Oklahoma, the ceremonial grounds of the Loyal Shawnee. "Sit down," Carole told me. "You're not Indian enough to dance." She, of course, danced merrily around the drum.

True, I do not look Indian. I am blonde and have blue eyes. Also true is that the amount of Indian blood in my veins is minute, as these things are measured; but it was not just that with Carole. It was the Cherokee thing. To her way of thinking when we were children, the Loyal Shawnees, her father's tribe, were more exclusive than the Cherokees.

Indians can be as biased as anyone else. At another ceremonial dance near Ponca City, I watched an Osage father help dress his young son in tribal regalia. "Suck in your stomach," the father scolded. "You look like a Pawnee." Indians find this story very funny. Maybe not Pawnees, but I have never told it to a Pawnee.

I am an enrolled Cherokee, which means I am listed on tribal rolls, can vote in tribal elections, and can trace my heritage back to a great-great-grandmother coming over the Trail of Tears, and before that to

Nancy Ward, a famous Cherokee woman known as Beloved Woman. So can my cousin Carole, since we share the same grandfather, but her greater blood quota is from her full-blood Shawnee father. Then, too, claiming Nancy Ward as an ancestor is much like saying George Washington is a kinsman.

According to legend, "Cherokees are a stubborn people. As stubborn as the devil's pig, which will be neither driven nor led." I was determined to proclaim my Cherokee bloodline despite my cousin's threats. Oddly enough, none of her Indian friends asked me about my heritage. I was invisible to them. This has happened to me several times since then, being unnoticed in a crowd of Indians. It is a good lesson for a majority race—good to learn what it feels like.

If my cousin had been the one working in the Indian store, it would have been a different encounter. "Smudge sticks?" she would have said with a sneer. "Any port in a storm, huh, Blondie?" Well, maybe she would not have said this to a customer or a stranger, but she definitely would have said it to a mere cousin.

When we were grown and Carole had married a full-blood Kiowa, she had a baby they named Tahlo, which means "Boy." He was a chubby little brown baby with button eyes and a thatch of black hair that stood straight up like a duckling's tailfeathers. He was such a cute, cuddly baby that I wanted to squeeze him, but every time I picked him up, he cried.

"I'm sorry, Connie," Carole said, "but you're scaring him. You're the whitest person he's ever seen."

Here's the story of Creation, according to Carole Greenfeather:

> When God first created man, He took clay, molded it, and put it in the oven to bake, but He was impatient and took it out too early. "No," God said, shaking his head, "too pale." And that was the first white man.
>
> So He tried again. He molded clay and put it into the oven, but this time He left it too long. "Uh-oh," He said, "too dark." And that was the black man.
>
> So He tried a third time, molded clay, and put it into the oven, and this time when He took it out it was red. God smiled a big smile and said, "Ahh. Just right." And that was the Indian.

January 12 Is Answer Your Cat's Question Day

Cat Talk

I am quite cross with my cats these days and with good reason.

I have friends who have dogs, and when I visit them, the dogs come galumphing to the door, jumping and barking an enthusiastic greeting.

Cats are different. The doorbell rings and cats either scuttle off to hide or they creep in as softly as a whisper. They might ignore the guest disdainfully, sit contorted in the middle of the floor as they engage in lavish personal hygiene, or slide around the person sniffing curiously. This is usual cat behavior, the cat behavior I am familiar with.

But this week, two new friends visited me—people who have not met my cats—and the moment they stepped through the door, my cats poured into the living room and threw themselves on the people. On both occasions, cats hung on their legs and leapt to their chairs. They clung to these strangers like shipwreck survivors. The tabby cat named Lola even climbed into a guest's bag sitting on the floor and refused to come out.

The people were flattered by all this attention. They were delighted with the cats' sociability. They thought the cats charming. I know better.

I know that this phony behavior was really directed at me. The cats were saying with their theatrical feline body language, "Thank heavens you have arrived. We are cooped up in this house with Connie day in and day out until we are bored into a coma. We are starved for intelligent, stimulating conversation. We are so desperate for companionship worthy of us we are about to howl and claw the furniture. So, let's have a smell to see where you have been and what other cats you know."

This is how my cats present themselves to the world, like miserable little orphans in a Charles Dickens novel starved for affection and gruel.

It was most annoying, just as the cats intended it to be. I run my legs off day and night pampering and caring for these cats. I do not complain when their toy mice clog up the vacuum cleaner. I rearrange the furniture to please them and give them the best views. I buy them educational toys and designer collars. I read aloud to them from Emily Dickinson. Now I see that all my efforts are like pouring water on sand. Slathering attention on human strangers is their way of telling me, once again, that I do not measure up to their high standards of cat care.

The minute the guests left—after Lola had been pulled complaining from the bag and forced to stay behind with me—the cats drifted back to their usual posts of windowsills and tables overlooking the lawn. I always thought they were entertaining themselves by watching birds and squirrels, but now I know the truth. They are staring out the windows forlornly, as miserable as pioneers on the lonely prairie hoping for a passerby, praying that anyone will happen along—a peddler in a wagon, a neighbor on horseback, a gunslinger outrunning the posse—anyone to relieve the aching boredom of living with me.

The moral of this misadventure is that we think we know our cats like the rhythm of our own heartbeat. We think we understand their needs and their interests. We think we can predict their moral choices and their behavior in times of crisis. But we don't know. We are lucky if we know our own heart's desire. The cats in our life are familiar but always mysterious, like the people in our lives.

It also tells me that I should put forth more effort in being the interesting, entertaining human my cats would like for me to be. How embarrassing to be dismissed as a dullard by a tabby cat.

January 13 Is Blame Someone Else Day

Stop! I Don't Want to Share Your Pain

Has someone taped a sign on my back that says, "Tell me your troubles?" Suddenly, everywhere I go, I attract tales of woe.

I first noticed it last spring with a home renovation project. Every worker wanted to tell me his troubles with his truck or his tools or his boss or his hangover. *This must be an occupational thing,* I thought, and dismissed it.

Then last summer a clerk at a grocery store greeted me innocuously with, "How are you?"

"Very well, thank you," I answered, as cheery as a songbird. Was that ever the wrong thing to say!

"I wish I were well," she said. "This morning I lost twenty dollars. My last twenty dollars. All I had to buy groceries till Friday. I don't know what I'm going to do. I've asked everybody I know and no one has twenty dollars. And me a diabetic."

Maybe it's seasonal, I thought. But months later, in the dead of winter, I was in a pet store when a fellow leapt into the aisle in front of me and exclaimed, "Remember me?"

"How are you?" I replied, hedging for time and memory. It didn't matter. He had a story to tell and I was the audience to hear it.

"Three years," he said. "So sick I thought I would die. They took a tumor the size of your fist out of my head . . ." and he was off. It was a saga to rival the *Iliad*—a detailed account of fevers and convulsions and midnight ambulance rides. I couldn't take it. When he stopped to take a breath, I said he looked great now and bolted for the door.

I have read that we are becoming a confessional society of victims, virtually introducing ourselves to strangers with such revelations as, "Hi, I'm a recovering anorexic." I think it is true.

"How you doing?" I ask a passerby, just making conversation.

"Getting better," he says. "My wife ran off with the gym teacher."

At the post office, a stranger blurts out to me, "I've quit ovulating."

"So I hear you're getting married," I say to an acquaintance. "Yes," she coos. "I was an abused child but my Jonathan is helping me forget my pain."

More information than I want to know.

My life is similar to the scene in *Gone with the Wind* where Confederate soldiers, wounded and dead, are stretched as far as you can see. Except in my life's story, they are all sitting up and telling me where it hurts.

I don't understand it. I am not particularly patient or comforting. I do not exude sympathy. Granted, there was a time in junior high when I thought I wanted to be a nun, but that phase disappeared when I realized I would have to stop wearing liquid eyeliner. I am not cut out to hear the sorrows of the world. I am not the woman holding up the flame and proclaiming, "Give me your tired, your poor, your huddled masses . . ."

Maybe this conversational trend is part of the tell-all, tabloid-news times. Memoirs outsell novels these days, and many are stories of pain. The best ones are skillful, compassionate books: *Angela's Ashes* by Frank McCort, *America Chica* by Marie Aranda, or *Paula* by Isabel Allende. The worst ones are like window-peeking at the trailer park.

I like memoirs, but my favorites are the funny ones. James Thurber's wide-eyed stories of "The Night the Bed Fell" or "The Day the Dam Broke." Debby Bull's hilarious book about lost love, titled *Blue Jelly.* She knew she had hit bottom, she wrote, when she identified with the song "I'm So Miserable Without You, It's Almost Like I've Got You Back."

If we are not sharing our pain, we are inflicting it. At a bookstore, a woman volunteered, "Boy, you're sure not as glamorous in person as your photograph, are you?" At the church coffee hour, a woman said to me, "I saw you on TV the other day. You looked washed out. Have you been sick? Was that an insect bite under your eye?" No, it was not a bug bite. What it was—and I did not tell her this—was an attempt at beauty. It was a mole I had darkened with mascara. I meant it to be a beauty mark.

"Oh, you know that TV lighting," I mumbled, throwing blame elsewhere.

Have we turned into a nation of crybabies? Can't we suffer in silence? Put on a happy face? Keep it to ourselves?

Where are the strong, silent heroes? The ones who climb back on the horse. Rub dirt on their wounds. The folks who pull the boots back on and lace them tighter. Where is John Wayne when we need him?

January 13 Is Make Your Dream Come True Day

Oh, How I Miss Frank Sinatra

Usually I am happy and optimistic, content with the day at hand. But I have to confess, there are those days—and those nights—when, oh, how I miss Frank Sinatra.

I have missed him sorely ever since I read Pete Hamill's elegant little book titled, *Why Sinatra Matters.* Hamill and Sinatra palled around in New York saloons in the 1970s. Sinatra matters, the writer says, because he represents the children of immigrants who transformed themselves and the country.

More than that, Sinatra matters because of his genius with the popular song, and because of his comeback after Ava Gardner. When he left his wife and three small children for her, his life started a tumble. He lost his recording contract, his movie career, and, for a while, even his voice. Ava taught him how to sing a torch song, the book says; she taught him the hard way.

But, Hamill writes, Sinatra got up. This is a reference to the prizefighters they both admired. The champs took the punches and were knocked down, but the great ones got up to fight another day. Someone told Sinatra what Dizzie Gillespie said, that a professional is the guy who can do it twice. Sinatra liked that. So Sinatra got up and rebuilt his career. He was a postwar hero, battered but wiser, like the character he played in the movie *Some Came Running.*

I miss the Sinatra era, when talent was real and hard work mattered. We did not begrudge entertainers their fame or money, because we thought they earned it. The press was different then. We admired celebrities because we did not know as much about them as we do today.

But that is not why I miss Sinatra. I know he represents a time when booze was glorified and women were trivialized, and I certainly do not miss that. I am selective in my nostalgia. What I miss is that lost age of glamour. It was the glamour of black dresses and jewelry, a glamour that seemed clearly defined and obtainable. We were young and on our way somewhere. We were beautiful and invincible. I miss all of that.

I saw Sinatra three times in Las Vegas, twice in concert and once in an exclusive restaurant at the top of Caesar's Palace. Sinatra and Dean Martin were there with a table of friends. Despite their reputations, nobody seemed drunk that evening, nobody got punched, and nobody was outrageous. But here's something you don't see every day. They had with them a big, burly guy who appeared to be their taster. Before they ate any dish, he tasted it—like the tables of the Roman emperors. Now that's a memory to haul out on gray, damp days and marvel at.

What I wore for the Las Vegas nights were little black dresses. And pearls. My hair was very short then and I was very thin. Across the dining room, just for an instant, Sinatra did a double take at me. I believe that for a split second he thought I might be Mia Farrow. I wasn't, and his flash of interest vanished.

Nobody else thought I looked like Mia Farrow. A Chinese friend mimed that I looked like a plucked and scalded chicken. The receptionist at the beauty salon begged me not to tell anyone where I had my hair done.

In that late Sinatra era, we danced close and we dressed up for parties. Christmas and New Year's Eve parties were extra dressy. Life was perfumed with a sense of romance and occasion.

On the blue days when I really miss Sinatra, I don't put on his torch songs. I put on his bright songs with Nelson Riddle: "I've Got You Under My Skin," "Anything Goes," and "You Make Me Feel So Young."

And then I get up. I know I will miss Sinatra again, but today, I get up, enjoy the music, and go on. That is a good message for the New Year: *I wish regeneration for us all and an everyday comeback like the champs.*

Fettuccine à la Sinatra

1 8-ounce package fettuccine
½ cup butter
½ cup whipping cream
¼ cup plus 2 tablespoons grated Parmesan cheese
Salt and pepper

Cook fettuccine until it is al dente. Drain pasta. While pasta is
cooking, make sauce by melting butter in a small saucepan on low
heat. Remove butter from heat; blend cream and cheese into it.
Return to heat and simmer thoroughly, season with salt and pepper.
Careful not to let the sauce come to a boil. Add the sauce to the
drained pasta and let stand, covered, for a couple of minutes.
Perhaps garnish with parsley.
    Serves three or four.

—From *The Sinatra Celebrity Cookbook: Barbara,
Frank, and Friends,* copyright 1996 by The Affiliates,
Barbara Sinatra Children's Center at Eisenhower
Medical Center, Rancho Mirage, California.

January 21 Is Martin Luther King Jr.'s Birth Date

Culture Shock

In front of the U.S. Embassy in Pretoria, South Africa, stands a bust of Martin Luther King with this inscription: *A just law is a man-made code that squares with the moral law or the law of God. An unjust law is a code that is out of harmony with the moral law.*

I was in South Africa working on a book. Many people travel to South Africa for safari, but the only animals I saw were a calico cat, a fuzzy white dog, and some brown cattle. I traveled with a party of scholars and spent most of my time in meetings trying to see how the new democracy is growing after apartheid.

I suffered mightily from jetlag, which disappeared only when I had a hearty African meal of oxtail, potatoes, and vegetables. The host was Mangosuthu Gatcha Buthelezi, chief of the Zulu tribe and now minister of home affairs. Our meal began with a long blessing in the tribal language, and then the chief said with a chuckle, "We assume that God speaks Zulu."

The first democratic elections in the nation's history were not held until 1994. Apartheid had been the official racist policy of South Africa since 1948. What I saw was a country scrambling to create a new nation. One man said this is what it must have been like in the United States in 1776. I met overworked public administrators trying to revamp a nineteenth-century British civil service and build an infrastructure to deliver basic services such as water, education, a treasury, transportation, and health. A new member of Parliament, a fiery labor organizer in her salad days, told me, "We were so busy fighting for democracy, we didn't stop to think how we would deliver democracy once we won it."

I visited the grave of martyred Steve Biko and the home of Afrikaner hero Johan Heynes of the Dutch Reformed Church. I stood in the kitchen while Mrs. Heynes prepared tea and told me about the Guy Fawkes Day when she and her husband sat in the family room playing gin rummy with grandchildren at their feet and fireworks outside. She turned to her husband and saw that he had been shot in the head. Assassinated.

I discovered South African jazz with its special sweet soul and became a fan of Abdullah Ibrahim. I learned the three-part handshake of the South African Community Party that once meant "comrade" and now means "friend." Despite the news reports of high crime, pandemics of disease, and the uphill obstacles facing them, the people I met were optimistic, smiling, and completely committed to the work of building a nation. Everyone I talked to for any length of time—Africans, Afrikaners, Coloureds, Indians, and English-speakers—all expressed a deep love, almost a reverence, for their country and a belief in its bright future.

I met South African heroes of the struggle: men and women who had been banned, exiled, jailed, or imprisoned on Robben Island with Nelson Mandela for decades. They were priests, lawyers, nurses, educators. I met former student revolutionaries, firebrand trade union leaders, and members of the Truth and Reconciliation Commission who told me that between 1960 and 1994, South Africa had suffered more deaths than the genocide of World War II.

South Africa is a country of contrasts: stretches of golden beaches, and not fifteen miles away, four hundred thousand people, mostly of East Indian descent, living in what is euphemistically called "temporary housing"—acres of shacks cobbled together of paper and scraps of lumber and tin. The education director in one province said his responsibility includes 6,500 schools and two million students. What he needs, immediately, is eighty thousand teachers.

Water is what is needed in other parts of the country. In the green hills near East London, a new dam and reservoir have changed lives. A young Afrikaner engineer, Corrie Smit, guided us through the area of new water. Miles of need stretch before him, but he knows the magnitude of the work he has accomplished. He drove us to tiny villages where a single water pump stands pristinely. Individual homes do not have water, but the water pump in the village is treasured. In nearby villages, women must carry water in plastic pails on their head from a water hole. I saw cattle standing in the water hole. Some women spend ninety minutes a day carrying water. Of course, it takes more time and more energy if the women are sick with tuberculosis.

In one village, Cecelia Kaulela invited us into her home, asked us to sign the village guest book, and told us about the changes in her life since the elections of 1994. Electricity, telephones, and the dirt roads have been upgraded. Most important, though, is the water. Not only is it easily accessible to her from a pump in the village, but it is also cleaner, so the health of her family has improved. We sat around her dining room table; a picture of the Lord's *Last Supper* hung above us on the wall. The Lord and His disciples are white. Cecelia and the rest of the villagers are black.

Her house is poor but spotless. Lace curtains flutter at the open windows. In the absence of running water in her home, the toilet is a privy outside. In the next room, three small children lounged on torn furniture and watched television. Before we continued our hot journey, Cecelia offered us something precious: Would you like to have a glass of water? she asked.

A few days later, I boarded a plane for a twenty-six-hour flight home. My seatmate was a young man from Southern California who is a stockbroker but who wants to be a TV sportscaster. He has a girlfriend named Tiffany, and he cannot believe that Meg Ryan left Dennis Quaid for Russell Crowe. In all the time I was in South Africa, I never once thought about Meg Ryan's love life.

This is a quote from Katherine Mansfield: "How hard it is to escape from places. However carefully one goes, they hold you. You leave bits of yourself fluttering on the fences—little rags and shreds of your very life."

We also carry with us little scratches and scars of the places we have been.

February

White as an Indian Pipe
Red as a Cardinal Flower
Fabulous as a Moon at Noon
February Hour—

—Emily Dickinson, poem 1250

February 12 Is Be Humble Day

Post Office Laments

Don't you love the way the universe invents ways to keep us humble? Just about the time I'm feeling pretty pleased with myself, along comes one of life's great levelers. A high school reunion is a big one.

It is impossible to impress or bamboozle people who knew you when you were six years old. Many of us arrive with old school pictures and moldy grudges itching to be settled. At least John Paul DeLozier had the kindness to apologize when I told him I had hated him for twenty years for nicknaming me Turnpike in the seventh grade. "Turnpike," he would say, "not a curve in sight."

Another great leveler is my neighborhood post office. Because of my business I am at the post office often, so you would think I could get over the frustration of no parking and long lines. But ask John Paul DeLozier how easily I get over things.

Monday morning there I was, in line at the post office but determined to move myself to a higher plane. I have not been studying yoga and meditation all these years for nothing. First, I stood squarely—*tadasana,* "standing mountain pose." I closed my eyes and began to breathe the relaxing *udasna,* "sounding breath." Standing like a mountain, eyes closed, sounding breath—getting calm and centered.

Then I opened my eyes, turned to the woman behind me in line, and said, "Why in the hell can't they open two lines?" In a flash I had a knot of people whipped into a white froth.

Then something interesting happened. Once our complaints about the service at the post office slowed, we segued into complaining about our health and various body parts. And then we began to exchange—contrast and compare—remedies, therapies, and medication. We were a cluster of women talking about tendonitis, inflamed fascia, ibuprofen, and ice/heat therapy. Another five minutes and we would have moved on to gynecology. Conversation with women usually does.

In that moment (several moments, actually, because the line seemed to be freeze-framed and not moving at all), the post office was transformed into an old general store. We were a bunch of neighbors in from the farms and villages to pick up provisions. All we needed was a country set decoration—crates of baby chicks, sacks of beans, bolts of yard goods, a potbellied stove.

According to Hinduism, life is divided into four stages. The first stage is that of a student, and our main responsibility is to learn. The second stage is householder, attending to marriage, family, vocation, and civic duty. The third stage is retirement from social obligations and working out a philosophy beyond the natural world, and the fourth stage is letting go of everything.

Maybe I am stuck in the wrong Hindu stage. Maybe what I ought to be doing is wandering in the forest with a begging bowl. Instead I am standing in line at the post office, being humbled another way.

One of my favorite literary stories is about William Faulkner, supposedly fired from his job at the post office in Oxford, Mississippi, because he would not always open the window to give the people their mail. He explained it this way: "All my life I'm going to be at the beck and call of some s.o.b., but I don't have to be at the beck and call of every s.o.b. with three cents to buy a stamp."

February Is Responsible
Pet Owners Month

I Met This Guy

"I met this guy, who looked like he might be a hatcheck clerk at an ice skate rink, which he turned out to be . . . ."

No, that's the wrong story. That's the start of a Lorie Anderson song I like.

My story begins this way:

I met this guy who was orange and white with four white feet and a head as round as an apple. I was working out of town and staying at a bed-and-breakfast. The first time I saw him, he was sitting on a cement bench by the alley, washing his face and trying valiantly to keep up appearances. It was clear that he had known better days, but this day he was thin and scruffy and not well.

"Does that cat live here?" I asked the innkeeper.

"No," she said, "but he's been hanging around for weeks. I don't feed him because I want him to go back where he came from. Every morning I tell him 'Go home,' but he keeps coming back, lying at the kitchen door."

I went inside and called someone with a local animal rescue organization. He said, "I'll give you a number to call at our shelter, but they're closed now. Call them tomorrow between ten and three."

For about the hundredth time I felt that I not only had been abducted by aliens but was living among them.

Where would the cat be the next day between the hours of ten and three? What could I do with a lost cat until then?

I could have asked, "Doesn't your animal rescue group rescue animals?" but I knew the answer: Yes, but they are full.

And I could have said to the innkeeper—what? What could I say that the orange-and-white cat hadn't already said?

The cat had said, "I don't speak your language. All I can do is lay down at your feet and hope that you see that I am hungry and sick and lost and scared. You're strong, so I hope you help me."

I cannot say it any better than that. So I scooped up the cat and drove back to Tulsa with him. I have never known a cat to lie on my lap in a car for more than ten minutes, but he lay on my lap the whole way, two hours.

When we got home and he met the resident cats, some of us hissed and spat, but we all squeezed together and made room for one more. I got him medical attention and good nutrition and a safe, warm place to live, and he doubled his weight. I thought he needed a special name, something regal to help him regain his dignity. So I named this orange-and-white cat Louie—after the French king Louis XIV, the Sun King.

Just when we had all adjusted to this new feline member of the household and I was feeling smug and proud of myself, I was hurrying along a downtown street on my way to a party. Carrying a vase of flowers. I turned into the wrong doorway and jumped back because there, just off the sidewalk, was a man, curled up. He had seen better days. He was scruffy and thin and looked sick.

"Sorry," I said. "Excuse me." And I backed away. Fast. And hurried on to the party.

The man in the doorway did not say anything. He just lay there, at my feet.

I would rather remember how I rescued the orange cat. That was a better day.

February 14 Is Valentine's Day

Love and Blackbirds, Bye Bye

I find Valentine's Day a time to be grateful.

I am grateful it is not still January. I am grateful I am finally over my head cold. I am grateful for the seductive displays of candy and flowers that I can't resist and for the brave postwinter flashes of color. Saucy reds and pinks make me happy.

I am grateful that I am not still in the fourth grade when the class valentines box was opened for all to see. We could measure our popularity by how many valentines we got. I got mountains of valentines in the fourth grade. These days my cat Muriel gets more valentines than I do.

I am grateful that I don't care how many valentines I get.

Serious romance is a rough river to navigate. I was reading something by a woman explaining her single life. "All the men I love," she wrote, "are either married, gay, or dead."

And I love Valentine's Day because of the poetry that surfaces and takes our hearts on romps and remembrances. I love romantic poetry, but I used to love a different kind. I used to love poetry about the height and depth and breadth my soul can reach. Then, Carl Sandburg's *Honey and Salt*. Then, Rod McKuen. That was back when I thought heartbreak was something chic, like wearing a little black dress. Once I had my heart broken, I found out there is nothing glamorous to it. It is like being sick in public.

Well, everything changes. Us, too, and if we are lucky, we know it.

Robert Frost said that poetry is a way of taking life by the throat. That is why I like a poetry anthology titled, *Bleeding Hearts: Love Poems for the Nervous and Highly Strung*. The poems are funny, sassy, tender, and throat-clutching. The poem "Goddamn the Empty Sky" is a poem about raw heartache by Chilean poet Violeta Parra. The poem damns the empty sky and stars at night and the ripply bright stream and everything else warm or beautiful all because, the refrain says, "my pain's as bad as that."

One of my favorite poems, "Casabianca," is by Elizabeth Bishop.

> Love's the boy stood on the burning deck
> trying to recite, "The boy stood on
> the burning deck." Love's the son
> stood stammering elocution
> while the poor ship in flames went down.
>
> Love's the obstinate boy, the ship,
> even the swimming sailors, who
> would like a schoolroom platform, too,
> or an excuse to stay
> on deck. And love's the burning boy.

One Valentine's Day I put that poem on the cover of homemade valentines. None of my friends knew what it meant. Me, either. I like that poem because it is so circuitous and confounding. Like love itself.

It reminds me of my favorite Chinese adage about love: "One tear met another tear floating down the river. Said the first tear, 'I'm the tear of a woman who lost her lover.' Said the second tear, 'I'm the tear of the woman who found him.'"

Ah, yes. I have been both women, and I have been both tears. I have been the river. And I will be again. And so I love Valentine's Day.

February is also National Wild Bird Feeding Month. I have developed an affection for blackbirds, especially starlings (the Sturnidae family). These birds do not hop; they walk on legs that turn from brown to bright pink during mating season. Think how interesting it would be if humans changed colors during mating; we would know so much more about one another. I love the starling's romantic nature. Males sometimes decorate a love nest with flowers, then woo females inside with song, much like a troubadour outside a damsel's window. Adult starlings eat insects and grain, but juveniles have a particular fondness for cherries. I told a four-year-old this, and he asked, "I wonder if that makes their tongues pink?"

In winter, from my window I see scattered starlings sitting silently, black ornaments in bare trees, and in the spring I watch them strut across greening lawns looking for bugs. In the autumn twilight, however, the aerial pyrotechnics of starling flocks are breathtaking. One evening in downtown Tulsa, just as the sun was setting in smears of gold and saffron, enormous swarms of them came in to roost. They left the fields where they were feeding, and one group after another joined the huge flock that was circling overhead. The flock circled, looped, cut sharply left and then right, and spiraled into figure-eights. Each arriving cluster melted into the greater flock. After about twenty minutes, the sky was flecked with black. Then, when all seemed to have gathered, the great flock—thousands of starlings—circled in one direction and suddenly descended as a whole into four trees, as smoothly as drawing a shade. The birds chittered noisily for a few moments, saying their prayers and goodnights, and went to bed for the night. Below the starlings, as night darkened, musicians and singers in formal black-and-white attire filed into a cathedral to perform the "Coronation Mass." What a creative fulcrum; day ended with the black starlings' spectacular flight, and night began with the tuxedoed musicians playing Mozart.

I like blackbirds in nature and I like them in art. If three can be considered a collection, then I have a little collection of Zuni blackbird fetishes carved of black marble with turquoise eyes. Each is no larger than a thimble. They are more than tiny works of art. A fetish has a spirit and magic power. These small stone birds are supposed to give me aid and protection and, since some are ravens, maybe a splash of witchcraft.

What is the difference between a fetish and a carving? "If you believe it is a fetish, it is," according to Mark Bahti's book *Spirit in the Stone.* That explanation is much like Mr. Hedley's lecture in literature class my sophomore year in college. "What is the difference between verse and poetry?" he asked the class. We sat like stone carvings ourselves, lumps of students without either magical or intellectual power, so he answered his own question. "Anyone can write verse," he said, "but only a poet can write poetry." We nodded solemnly at this arabesque answer. *A mystery,* we thought, *and clever us to know it is a mystery.* Not all questions can be answered in black and white. Much as J.R.R. Tolkien said, "Not all those who wander are lost."

Blackbirds appear often in literature. They pop up in nursery rhymes ("Four and twenty blackbirds baked in a pie") and in counting rhymes: "One for sorrow, two for mirth, three for a wedding, four for a birth."

In poetry they are stark images, from Wallace Stevens' "Thirteen Ways of Looking at a Blackbird" to Basho's haiku:

> A lone crow
> sits on a dead branch
> this autumn eve.

The quoting raven is menacing in Edgar Allen Poe's poem, but in Native American stories, the raven is a trickster and a creator. According to American Indian legend, the raven brought salmon to eat, water to drink during a drought, and fire from the sun so humans would not freeze. As a trickster, he taught humans to enjoy life.

In Christian literature, ravens symbolize God's providence because it was a raven that fed the prophet Elijah. In Christian art, ravens often appear with St. Oswald, St. Benedict, and St. Paul the Hermit.

Still, a raven is often considered a bird of ill omen, associated with death and bad luck. A crow represents discord and strife. Perhaps that is why an assemblage of crows is known as a murder—a flock of birds, a murmur of starlings, but a murder of crows.

Ravens and crows are not literally black; they are iridescent green, blue, or purple. In just the right angle of sunlight, their black plumage shines like oil. Ravens were not always black, according to Roman legend. Once they were as white as swans, but when a raven told Apollo that the nymph he loved was unfaithful, the god not only shot him with an arrow but also turned him black forever more.

"To eat crow" refers to an act that is humbling or disagreeable; to travel "as the crow flies" is to move in a straight line and the shortest distance between two points. The term "Jim Crow" grew from a popular minstrel song to become the catchphrase for segregation.

One moment I was noticing blackbirds; the next thing I knew, my interest had leapt like a prairie fire from mild affection to obsession.

Bleary eyed I searched books and the Internet in a quest to know more about ravens and crows. Both birds, I discovered are members of the genus *Corvus* and the Corvidae family, which is an extended family of big, noisy songbirds: jays, magpies, nutcrackers, and choughs. My study developed into corvidophilia, the love of crows and ravens. Not everybody feels this way toward blackbirds. "I'm so mad I could spit," a woman said in a plant store. "Blackbirds keep swooping down and eating all the dusty miller out of my garden." I wonder if Poe on that midnight dreary was pondering weak and weary about death or if he suffered from corvidophobia, the fear of corvids.

I learned that ravens are the larger of the two, the size of a hawk, and have a pointed tail. Crows are pigeon-sized with a rounded tail. Corvids are known as intelligent birds, brighter than cats, dogs, and monkeys. They are not depicted as clever birds in the Aesop fable "The Raven and the Fox" (sometimes titled "The Crow and the Fox" by people who are not corvidophiles). In that children's story, a raven loses the cheese it holds when it succumbs to a fox's charm and opens its beak to sing. The moral of the tale: *Do not trust flatterers.* In the children's story "The Crow and the Water," however, a bright crow raises the water level in a jug high enough to drink it by dropping stones into the water.

The more I read, the more I liked these mysterious birds. I began to wonder if I possess a corvidophile personality. If so, according to one aviary website, I am odd and a nonconformist, I wear black clothes and strange hair colors, I love words and etymology, and I quote poetry or from old movies. *Could be me,* I think. I read on; some corvidophiles "affect accents or caw randomly during conversation." Whew. That lets me out. I have never, to my knowledge, cawed during a conversation. I have made plenty of other sounds of derision—snorts, sniffs, groans, and rude plosive noises, but never an outright caw. But then I never thought about it. Now that I have, maybe I'll try it.

An old folksong about blackbirds existed long before the Lennon/McCartney song ("Blackbird singing in the dead of night . . ."). My favorite musical blackbird is in the song "Bye Bye Blackbird," which is largely why I was drawn to blackbirds in the first place. But what does that song mean? According to my research, the song was written in 1926 and refers to a lady who was leaving the big city and going home to her mother. Blackbird might be another term for the johns in the city or it might be slang for the city itself. Chicago? One thing was certain. The lady—sad and disillusioned—was out of there. Melodic and memorable, the song is as puzzling as Elizabeth Bowen's poem about love. The song's second verse is about bluebirds!

Perhaps blackbirds, like love, should not be analyzed too closely. Maybe I like blackbirds just because they are easy to see and I am nearsighted. Maybe I will just accept the fact that I love red hearts and blackbirds and leave it at that.

February Is International Twit Award Month

Imagine My Surprise

There was a death in my family recently, so there was a big family gathering. You know how there is always one person in the family who irritates everybody? Stirs everything up? Pushes everybody's fast-forward buttons? There is always one.

Well, imagine my surprise to discover that I'm the one. Me. I'm the one who is always late, always changing plans, dabbling in the arrangements, bossing people around.

My sister and I went to our hometown for the funeral, a small town where seasoned grudges lurked in the shadows and old grievances snapped at our heels like mean little dogs. Slightly hysterical from the extended family and too much fried chicken, one evening we sank into a movie and watched *Gosford Park*.

Oh, sweet relief, I thought. *The secrets and snideness of fictional strangers.* Just then my sister looked at me with astonishment. "That's you!" she said.

"Who?" I asked. "Which one?"

"Both of them."

According to her, I am the character played by Maggie Smith—fey and flighty. Except during family gatherings, and then I am also the Helen Mirren character—barking orders at people and running a tight ship.

Surprising, isn't it, how people see us? That is, how inaccurately they see us. How ignorant and misguided even our family and friends can be.

In high school, my dearest friends and I played a game in which we compared one another to flowers. Which were we most like: (a) a long-stemmed red rose, (b) a violet, or (c) a common field daisy? I could accept being a delicate violet, but I knew in my heart that my inner flower is a long-stemmed red rose. My friends all saw me as the common daisy. I sulked for years about that.

Then I realized, *sometimes people are wrong.* Even our closest friends. Especially our family and childhood friends. They don't see our true selves. They don't know the person we grow to be. They see only the awkward, gobbling chick and not the soaring meadowlark we become.

My birthday, this year, came on the heels of the hubbub of the funeral. After grief and loss and little-town blues, I stood at the curb to welcome the birthday with open arms. My current friends would make things right. My wise and wonderful friends would shower me with attention and chase away the family blues. Last year, florists streamed in with bouquets of flowers, the postman staggered with bags of birthday cards and packages from friends afar. Oh what joy, to be so loved.

So this year, I was ready. I had a stack of dollar bills to tip the parade of florists. I set out a big silver bowl to hold the pile of birthday cards. And I waited. I got a birthday card from a politician running for office and one floral delivery from my godcat Topaz, a thoughtful green-eyed cat. Then the birthday seemed to run aground. Finally I called the florist and asked coyly if anything was coming my way.

"Nooo," she said after a long pause. "Should there be?" I gathered up my one-dollar bills and took myself to the movie to see the exquisite Cate Blanchett portraying a strong, adventurous woman.

There are never enough birthday messages, are there, to make up for being likened to *Gosford Park* characters and a field daisy when we see ourselves as roses and Cate Blanchett?

Well, sometimes we are all wrong. Just last week I had symptoms of an approaching migraine. Not auras exactly, but eyesight blurrier than usual and trouble with light. That is a sure sign of a migraine. Except this time it wasn't. Turned out I had my contacts in the wrong eyes. Sometimes we are wrong, even about ourselves.

February Is Return Carts to Supermarket Month

Stress!

I hope I am not talking to you when I bring this up, but I want to talk about stress. Not the people who get it—the people who give it. The folks out there who transmit stress like a horde of Typhoid Marys.

For example, the grocery store parking lot. Recently I was dodging wind and rain and hurrying to load groceries into the trunk when I heard and felt a loud wham! A runaway grocery cart had crashed into my car, breaking the headlight. Nobody was in sight, but the parking lot was littered with grocery carts scattered like children's toys.

What sort of people jump into their cars and leave their empty grocery cart to go on a wild rampage? The same people who drop paper towels on the floor in ladies' rooms, I guess. Do we need parking lot patrols to ticket them or a great mother in the sky to pick up after them?

A memorable book, *Nickel and Dimed,* documents the efforts of a woman working at low-wage jobs. In one job, she tried to live on the seven dollars an hour she made at Wal-Mart, where her job day in, day out was refolding and rehanging women's clothes. Why do women scatter the garments like that? she wondered. She concluded that the shoppers were all mothers who spend their days picking up after children, so the clothing department was the only place they could act like spoiled kids themselves.

Could be. Then they move on to the parking lot and fire shopping carts at my car.

I think the way we handle stress depends on gender. Men calm their nerves by buying power tools. Women buy shoes. I have almost two dozen pair of shoes in my closet. I don't apologize. Unlike men and their power tools, shoes are quiet and I know how to use them.

In the same grocery store parking lot, I watched a grown man load his groceries into his pricey car and then deliberately push the empty cart as hard as he could across the lot. He stood and watched it bounce off a curb. I could have let it go at that, but I didn't.

"Excuse me," I shouted. "Why did you do that?"

"Huh?"

"I want to know why you did that."

"Mind your own business."

I stood my ground. I said that it *was* my business, that I shop here, that runaway carts have damaged my car and that they are dangerous.

His wife kept urging him to get into the car and stop yelling at me, and eventually he did. He spun out of the lot with a final repartee of logic and maturity: "Maybe when they lower their prices I'll take their goddamned carts back in."

Grade school playgrounds are full of kids like him.

Coping with stress is as slippery as juggling goldfish. I know a woman who is a social worker for delinquent teens. Her hobby, she told me, is to work weekends at a horse barn. "Exercising the horses?" I asked. "Teaching riding?"

"No," she replied, "my greatest satisfaction is mucking out the horse barns." Then she explained. "I work with delinquent teens," she said. "Most of them are repeat offenders. Their home situations are horrific. All day long I deal with crap. That's why when the weekend comes, I go to the horse barn and shovel horse manure. When I move crap there, it stays put."

Interesting philosophy.

In a similar but lesser vein, here is a tip I just learned: wig tape. Double-sided wig tape. Useful for accessories, such as holding scarves in place and to keep choker necklaces from slipping or bra straps from showing.

Sadly, it will not keep grocery carts in place. Wig tape is not a monumental discovery, just a little something to help with life's small frustrations. On days when we feel we are floundering in the world of stress, when nothing we do stays put, when everything seems to be sliding out of control, those are the days that we are grateful for any advice.

This is it for today: wig tape.

February 17 Is Random Act of Kindness Day

Elegy for an Ant

I

A woman stood in my kitchen rhapsodizing about how love had changed her life.

She waved her arms in the air, so that the just-out-of-the-box diamond flashed on her left hand. Love with Edgar, she proclaimed, had plucked her from a miserable life of single evenings and tables for one—and here she looked at me with pity. Love with Edgar had rescued her from a solitary middle age and transformed her into a gentle, caring person. Then, with that selfsame hand, she smashed an ant on my kitchen counter and flicked it to the floor.

"That was my ant," I said.

"What?"

"That ant lived here. I loved that ant."

She remembered urgent business elsewhere and cut her visit short.

II

A young woman in a doctor's reception room ignored me and talked on her cell phone about her longing heart. "Me and Tyrone went to see *The Wedding Singer* and I cried all the way through it. I'm like, 'Oh I want that to be me.' Or—wait!—was that me and Keith?"

III

Ah, February, the red month—all lipstick, roses, and hot blood.

Sometimes I think, "What was *that* all about?"

My favorite book of love poems these days includes "Poem about Heartbreak That Go On and On" by June Jordan. This is the poem in its entirety:

bad love last like a big
ugly lizard crawl around the
house
forever
never die
and never change itself
into a butterfly.

On the sugary end of the spectrum, I read *Growing Myself: A Spiritual Journey through Gardening,* by Judith Handelsman. The concept is that plants have spirits we can communicate with, but we must be gentle and remember our manners. Ask, "Who wants to come into the house?" before we cut blossoms. Warn a plant before it is pruned. Ask a rootbound plant to help when you are repotting it. Thank a dying plant for its life. If we do this, the plants will respond. Not in words, probably, but they will flourish and so will we. This book has convincing anecdotal evidence for someone who needs little convincing. I read it and immediately gave my plants names: Penelope, Albert, Danno, Ruby. Now I try to remember to speak politely to them each day. Nothing wants to be ignored.

Nuala O'Faolain's forceful memoir of a Dublin woman, *Are You Somebody?* tells of her different loves: family, books, career, romance, passion. Finally, it tells of how she came to love herself as a mature woman.

"I'd read somewhere," she wrote, "that if you watched a year's television, only three percent of the human faces you would see would be those of women over, say, fifty or fifty-five; older women only figure on television in ads and soap operas." So she produced an award-winning television series of elderly Irish women looking into the camera and telling the story of their lives.

Now, as an older woman herself, she has found things to love besides lovers: health, landscapes, friends, food and drink, books, music, a cat, and a dog.

This gooey month, I'll think of all the things I love: peaches, pears, watermelon, and strawberries in season; being able to light the water heater; remembering to clean the filter before the air conditioner stops working; veterinarians who make follow-up phone calls and mean it; people who listen when I talk to them; a sense of humor; kindness; old ladies; the color yellow; and good friends.

A good friend is someone like Hilary. I called her and said, "I've just assembled a new desk chair all by myself and have only one piece left over," and she said, "That piece wasn't important anyway."

IV

Flies, cockroaches, and some people do not stir my heart, but I love the nameless ants.

March

We like March.

His shoes are Purple—

—Emily Dickinson, from poem 1213

March 2 Is Old Stuff Day

Whither the Wimple

I wish the wimple would come back in fashion.

Or the barbette. Or, at the very least, the snood.

These are all historic hair coverings, and could I ever use them. There are days when no matter what I do to my hair—curl, back comb, fluff, style, spray—I leave the house looking like Mamie Eisenhower.

Some women save the day with a ball cap, but I am not a ball cap woman. Ball caps make me resemble a cranky goose.

My hair is too short for a snood, which is sort of a crocheted hair net that was popular in the 1940s. No, what I need is the wimple from medieval times. Eleanor Aquitaine wore a wimple—a cloth draped under the chin, fastened at the top of the head, and topped with a fabric circlet like a crown.

Plus, the wimple would hide excess chins.

For chins alone, I could fall back on the simple barbette, another fashion from the fourteenth century. The barbette is a strip of cloth that goes under the chin and over the ears to the top of the head. I think a veil is involved, too, but perhaps that is optional.

My friend Lynn commiserated with me. "I know what you mean," she said. "When our hair looks good we just feel better about ourselves."

Few things can drag us down like bad hair. A fever blister perhaps, or a sty in the eye, but those are an act of God. Ugly hair seems like character weakness.

I come by this fussiness genetically. I attribute it to my Aunt Ila, my favorite aunt, who has two passions in life. One is decorating the family cemetery plot. She used to make the floral wreaths—crepe paper flowers dipped in wax. Now she buys them, sturdy plastic flowers that have little resemblance to real plants either in shape or in color. One year her floral tributes were plastic bouquets the color of café latte. She stuck them helter-skelter into the ground on long bare stems. The effect was a brown surreal landscape.

My Aunt Ila's other interest is decorating herself. In the 1930s and 1940s, she was a great beauty with dark eyes and dark hair. She had movie star glamour, much like Hedy Lamarr. Aunt Ila is in her nineties and still devotes her days to shopping for clothes, applying her makeup, and dyeing her hair. She has a fey eccentricity that makes her, without intending to be, the funniest person in the family. I have a wonderful photo of her at a family gathering with a blond wig on backwards. When I showed it to her she said, "Oh dear, look at the wrinkles on my hands." Her hospital call to another relative is family lore. "Gene had the same thing you have," Aunt Ila told the sick relative. "I visited him and he died three days later."

I am a great fan of author Carolyn See, her novels and her memoir. She teaches creative writing at UCLA and conducts writing seminars. Her book *Making a Literary Life: Advice for Writers and Other Dreamers* is just like being in her writing seminar. Our friends and family, she writes, will become the characters in our books. They will be our heroes and our villains, even if we write about fifteenth-century France. Aunts and uncles are our artistic material, she says. "This is where your treasure lies. God deals us a hand full of kings, queens, knaves and aces."

We are all characters in one another's stories.

Shakespeare had his heroes and tragedies; he had Henry V and Hamlet. I have my own. I have Aunt Ila and I have my troublesome hair. What I do not have is a wimple.

March Is National
Women's History Month

Nelly Bly

When I was in the sixth grade, my life changed, all because of the alphabet.

Until then, our school classes had been divided alphabetically. I went from the first to the fifth grade with about twenty *A–G* kids. Then, in the sixth grade—oh, trauma!—we were mixed up with *H–Z* kids. Kids I didn't even know. A mob of strangers, a horde—probably *sixty* of them.

One day in social studies class, we moved our chairs into a circle, and the teacher asked us what we wanted to be when we grew up. A girl across the room said she wanted to be a writer. What nerve! It was like saying you wanted to be Miss America or Queen of the May. I wanted to be a writer, too, but I would never have said it aloud. That girl—whose name started with an *M*—had spoken my dream. When it came my turn, I said I wanted to be a lawyer like Perry Mason on TV, an alien idea that dropped into my head like a tiny meteorite.

Maybe the girl with an *M*-name emboldened me, because I went through college majoring in journalism and communication. My family did not care what I majored in as long as it wasn't acting, which I considered.

I did not develop much aptitude in domestic skills at that age, and none of the women in my family seemed to care about that either. My grandmother tried to teach me to crochet but gave it up as hopeless. My mother did teach me to iron white shirts, bake angel food cakes, and make meringue pies piled like cumulus clouds. Other than that, my sister and female cousins and I could learn to cook and sew and clean—or not. We were free to go our own ways. About the time I was graduating from college my mother suggested that I move back to my hometown and work at the bank, an idea outrageous enough to match the Perry Mason career goal. We looked at one another with matching baffled frowns—"Where did *that* come from?"—and never mentioned it again. She was not a stage mother pushing me into a profession, nor did she dote on my little accomplishments by pasting clippings or prizes in a scrapbook. She did want me to be independent. I was living at home and commuting to college when I nervously told her that a girl at the college had asked me to be her roommate and I was considering it. Leave home? How would my family accept such shocking news? "I'll help you pack," my mother said. "I believe in seeing the other side of the mountain," she often said.

Not that there were many mountains in northeastern Oklahoma. It is an old joke, but around my hometown, we knew we had proof that the world was flat. Once people crossed the county line and disappeared over the horizon, they were never heard from again.

So I became a journalist. I was pleased when the United States Postal Service issued stamps honoring four female journalists, trailblazers in what was a male profession: Ida Tarbell, a muckraking journalist who wrote investigative reports of Standard Oil in 1902; Marguerite Higgins, a foreign correspondent in the 1950s; Ethel Payne, the first lady of the black press, who wrote a famous article about the Alabama bus boycott in 1956; and my favorite—Nelly Bly.

Nelly Bly was born Elizabeth Jane Cochran in 1854 in Pennsylvania. She began her career writing a column about a woman's place for the *Pittsburgh Dispatch,* taking the pen name Nelly Bly from a popular song by Stephen Foster. Then she moved to New York to write for *The World.* Her first assignment was to feign insanity and be admitted to the Women's Lunatic Asylum to expose the poor treatment of patients in that hospital. In 1889 she became internationally famous when she set out to travel around the world in fewer than eighty days. She traveled by train, ship, rickshaw, and burro, and she made it—around the world in seventy-two days. Thanks to Nelly Bly, female reporters began writing hard news, not just fluffy features and society columns.

I am particularly fond of her because my grandmother's name was Nelly Bly. Nelly Bly Young. Don Carlos became her married name. My grandmother did not go around the world. She raised a big family in a small town through the Depression. Sometimes she hoed strawberries for hire to feed her family. Later she was a cook at the school cafeteria. During World War II, she had three sons and two sons-in-law in the service—five patriotic stars displayed in her window. She cooked three meals a day every day of her life, crocheted, quilted piles of handmade treasures, made the best strawberry shortcake I have ever tasted, and sang a mournful song about two poor little babes lost in the woods.

These female journalists and the women in my family made it possible for me to become my own person. I have not gone around the world in eighty days, either. I came to Tulsa and became a writer. However, here is something weird. My maiden name began with a *C* and I married twice, both times to men whose surnames begin with a *C*. I blame that on grade school, when I never knew anyone beyond the letter *G*. I am blessed by women, but I am haunted by the alphabet.

March 8 Is International Women's Day

No Way to Treat a Heroine

Am I the only one outraged at the business details revealed in the obituaries of Millie Benson? She is the author who wrote the first twenty-three Nancy Drew books under the pseudonym Carolyn Keene. Like many other women in this country, I grew up a great fan of Nancy Drew, girl detective, and like many women writers in this country, I grew up a fan of Carolyn Keene, the author of this wonderful series. It was not just the fictional character—it was the writer who was a heroine to me. Mystery writer Carolyn Hart, proclaimed as America's heir to Agatha Christie, says her career was inspired by the Nancy Drew series.

So I was horrified to learn that under her contract, Miss Benson was paid a paltry $125 a book, never received any royalties, and was prohibited from revealing her identity as the author. She only came to public notice in a 1980s lawsuit. The books she wrote have sold 100 million copies in seventeen languages.

Somebody was raking in the dough off of spunky, original Nancy Drew, but it sure wasn't the author. One hundred million copies and Ms. Benson received less than $3,000.

I do not care if that was the contract she signed and the business deal she made in the 1930s. It was wrong. There is a legal right and a moral, ethical right and this was not right. An honorable person—even an honorable publishing syndicate—would have stepped forward and said, "In gratitude and because of the unexpected and overwhelming success of this series, we want to revisit the contract." I do not argue that she should have been retroactively awarded the usual ten or fifteen percent royalty; even one percent would have increased her remuneration by, oh, a hundred million dollars or so.

This was no way to treat a heroine. Millie Benson was not a crybaby. She was a professional, one of the finest things that can be said about a writer, and she was a working journalist literally until the day she died in May 2002, at age ninety-six.

I don't want to hear about art as its own reward or all the other artists who sold their work for a song or who sold nothing in their lifetimes. Posthumous fame makes interesting biographies but not the life we want to live. I am going to wear a button that reads, "I want mine now." That means I want my applause, my gratification, and my royalty check now. Yesterday, if possible.

The story of Carolyn Keene reminds us that greed is a part of human nature, even my own. I bought my sister a first-edition Thornton W. Burgess book of animal tales from our childhood. Then I discovered that I love *Old Mother West Wind* and the *Merry Little Breezes* more than I love my sister, because I kept the book for myself and sent her a nightgown.

We are a shallow species and we have silly heroines. We wonder in print if Madonna is pregnant, if Stella McCartney disapproves of her father's marriage, and how poor Wynona Ryder will fare with her shoplifting charges. And we cheat the Carolyn Keenes.

I think we can do better. But then, I also think that someday Mr. Darcy will come striding up the lane to me, out of Regency England, wearing his fawn-colored trousers and his high boots, determined to confess his love. On that day, I will see that his pride and prejudice have melted into a gentle, caring—but very masculine—personality. He will be wealthy but generous. Ah, sweet fantasy.

And then all will be right with the world. Greedy publishers will get their just deserts and all the Carolyn Keenes will get their due rewards. We will get better heroines for our time than today's popular culture has to offer. And my sister might even get the book I bought for her. That's what I'll hope for. Tomorrow.

March Is Academy Awards Month

Oh, My Stars and Garters

I can't believe I watched all four hours of the Academy Awards. Even if I was ironing, or rebuilding the carburetor from my car, the awful truth is that was four hours of gawking at celebrities. I especially resent the time spent since my favorite movie did not win Best Picture and I hated Gwyneth Paltrow's dress.

It just shows me how insidious this cultural obsession with celebrity and fame has become. It is everywhere. I read in the local newspaper that actor Charlie Sheen was changing his name to Charles. This breaking news was issued by his agent, who also changed Ricky Schroder's name to Rick. I cannot believe someone sent this out as a news release, that a local newspaper printed it, and that I read it.

Take the thorny issue of *People* magazine. Refusing to buy it seems quite noble. I can't remember the last time I purchased a *People* magazine. December, I think. But only because it contained a great holiday recipe for sweet potatoes. Also, the story about Kate Moss was too long to read in the checkout line.

Does that high moral road also apply to the dentist's office? Can I read it there? And what about the slicker celebrity magazines, such as *Biography* and *Interview*?

And what about books? Let's see a show of hands of who wants to read another biography of movie stars who have found themselves? Not their rich and famous selves. No, their true, inner, fully evolved, emotionally healthy, intellectually astute, and shrewd business selves. Those selves.

Okay, now who wants just to read the juicy parts for free in newspapers and magazines? Me, too. But even I draw the line. Current celebrity biographies I have passed on include Goldie Hawn, Jane Fonda, Jerry

Lewis (oh, come on!), Bono (and I do not mean Sonny), and Donald Trump (yuck).

Yet, I confess . . . Just last week I was staying awake nights to finish the dual biography of Bobby Darin and Sandra Dee, which turned out to be painfully depressing. I was driven to it, I believe, by a special on public television. I hope I have learned once and for all not to let television be my true north of taste and judgment.

I have a crackpot theory that our fascination with celebrity is because we seem to know more about these people than we know about our neighbors or friends. I am shocked and feel slightly betrayed when I discover that people who have been friends for twenty years once had an abortion, or are adopted, or had a long childhood illness, and I did not know it. In this age of public confession, celebrities would tell us this personal stuff at the drop of a hat. They would bring their own hat.

It is interesting to see the changes in the biography genre over the years. For a book review I gave at the public library, I read a hefty five-hundred-plus-page biography of Rudolf Nureyev. This is a clear example of the style of biography currently popular—laboriously researched and every detail stacked on the page like bricks. I like the fact that biographies today are more honest and do not portray their subjects as gods on Mt. Olympus, but too many go overboard. They not only reveal a life, warts and all, but also they often reveal so many warts that even the prettiest subject begins to resemble the Elephant Man. This style of biography, someone said, gives death a new terror.

It was true of the Nureyev book. The research about his childhood in Russia was fascinating. He was born on a trans-Siberian train into a family of poor Tartar Muslims descended from Genghis Khan, and he grew up in a one-room mud hut in the town of Ufa, nicknamed the Devil's Inkpot because it was so muddy and dark. His father was a professional soldier who beat Nureyev whenever he caught the boy going to dance class. As a boy, Nureyev was frail, sensitive, blond, shabby, and unpolished. From childhood he had a fierce, driven determination to dance. "All my life," he said, "even as a boy in Russia, I had to grab life by the throat." This information is important for understanding the artist and adult he became.

Then the extensive detail about his homosexuality took over the book. Did I really want to know about all the promiscuous cruising, the casual sex, the call boys arriving during dinner, the flirtation with Mick

Jagger? Actually, I did, in a prurient way, but I did not need all of it to get the gist. In such biographies, I want to tell the author to use some judgment and do not give us every fact that is unearthed.

This reminds me of a story about Harry Truman when he was stumping for election and only one farmer showed up to hear his speech. "What do you want to do?" Truman asked, and the farmer replied, "Well, if I went out to feed my cattle and only one showed up, I believe I'd feed her." So Truman took a deep breath and delivered his speech. Then he asked, "What did you think?" The farmer thought a minute and then said, "Well, if I went to feed my cattle and only one showed up, I believe I'd feed her, but I don't believe I'd feed her the whole damn load."

My attitude toward celebrities may not be high-minded but it is selective. No wonder I found space in my wobbly moral stance to accommodate a passing fancy for celebrity recipes.

This began when I discovered the recipe for Frank Sinatra's linguini. It is easy and it is good. And then I found Oprah's deviled egg recipe—too much work, too many ingredients.

Suddenly a recipe addict, I made a search for celebrity cookbooks. I was fascinated by Jackie Kennedy's beef stroganoff and Bess Truman's apple pudding.

Famous Recipes by Famous People, published by the Hotel Del Monte in California in 1936, included recipes by Lynne Fontanne and Alfred Lunt, Sherwood Anderson, John Steinbeck, William Powell, and Gertrude Stein—whose recipe, like her poetry, had no punctuation. A note from Mrs. Franklin D. Roosevelt said the president's favorite Sunday night supper was scrambled eggs prepared on a chafing dish at the table.

Like a hobbit on a mission, I trekked on to discover *A Treasury of White House Cooking,* with recipes from almost every president and first lady from Washington to Nixon. Oh, the joy of it—Martha Washington's meatloaf and Calvin Coolidge's corn muffins. Dolly Madison, I read, was one of the liveliest of first lady hostesses. Instead of the president, it was she who sat at the head of the table. She rouged her cheeks, dipped snuff, and wore a feathered turban. Mrs. Madison was famous for her desserts, but she also served a wine soup made with veal knuckles and sherry.

The book includes whole White House menus for such occasions as a formal dinner for Princess Margaret and Lord Snowdon (boned squab for them), or to honor Duke Ellington (he got beef), or the president of Peru and his wife (a dinner that began with salmon mousse).

For something less historical, I turned to *The Sinatra Celebrity Cookbook*. The cookbook sales benefit a good cause, a child-abuse center, and many of the recipes were enticing, including Tony Bennett's lasagna and Peggy Lee's jade salad. An entire section of Mexican recipes includes Kirk Douglas' hot sauce and Johnny Cash's chili. Mr. Cash wrote that instead of chopped sirloin steak, he sometimes substituted snake meat.

Sharon Stone's zenlike recipe for pomme du jour is less carnivorous. Here it is: Walk to the refrigerator, open the door, open the fruit drawer, take out an apple, eat it. I guess that serves one.

Although the Sinatra cookbook was published in 1997, it shows us how transitory celebrity can be. Whom can I impress by making Ivana Trump's chicken paprika or Chuck Connors' Manhattan clam chowder?

Bess Truman's Apple Ozark Pudding

1 beaten egg
¾ cup sugar (or Splenda)
⅓ cup plain flour
⅓ teaspoon salt
1 ½ teaspoons baking powder
1 cup chopped and peeled apple
½ cup broken nuts (pecan or walnut)

Butter a pie dish. Preheat oven to 350 degrees. Add sugar to egg and beat well until creamy. Sift dry ingredients into mixture and beat until smooth. Fold in apples and nuts. Bake 20 minutes or until well browned. Will puff up during baking then fall. Top with vanilla ice cream or whipped cream.

Serves six.

—From *A Treasury of White House Cooking*, by
Francois Rysavy, as told to Frances Spatz Leighton
(New York: G. P. Putnam's Sons, 1972).

The Second Week of March Is National Procrastination Week

Mañana

I read that the average person spends 150 hours a year looking for things. That is almost four workweeks. Those people must have taken time-management classes. If I spent only 150 hours looking for things, I would nominate myself for a MacArthur Foundation genius grant.

Disorganization is an annoying character flaw. I have it, and it annoys me mightily. I shuffle again and again through piles of paper the way I keep bumping my knee on the edge of the desk. The actions are similar; both are repetitive and involve swearing.

I marvel at all whose lives move as methodically as an assembly line. My own life lurches along in fits and starts, heaps and piles, backtracking and bungling. It is a blur of bad habits, personality quirks, and wild-eyed Thurberesque phobias.

Disorganization is merely a pesky pup compared to the big dog that plagues my life—procrastination.

To minimize it, I made jokes about it. "If *Schoolhouse Rock* were still around," I said, "this could be the sequel to 'Conjunction Junction.'" I tried to write the song myself, a story song about taking a procrastination vacation, giving myself a procrastination citation, and celebrating with a procrastination libation.

I dismissed procrastination as a petty sin, akin to laziness, second cousin to sloth, until one day . . . I looked it up. In a panic I called my sister.

"I've got a new condition," I said, "and it's related to depression."

"Really? I've got a new bedspread. It's blue, too."

Forget sibling sympathy. I was on my own. Who would have thought there was so much information available about procrastination—websites, scholarly research, professional papers? The more I read, the worse I felt. The descriptive phrases blurred together: clinical depression, cognitive distortion, perfectionist expectations, neurotic avoidance, emotional instability, inability to delay gratification, lack of self-control, poor self-esteem, self-handicapping, extreme anxiety, obsessive compulsive disorder, sensitivity to rejection.

I do not take lightly the very real problems of emotional and mental disorders, but as I read on, I decided that my procrastination problem is not as serious as I had originally thought. Like other disorders, procrastination is wide ranging, but only one-fourth of procrastinators are chronically disabled by the condition. I choose to diagnose myself as mildly afflicted.

According to researchers, procrastination occurs among the general public and within the academic environment, especially among college students. Self-help tips include the following: (1) get an appointment book, (2) use it every day, (3) prioritize work, (4) plan realistically (which means do not underestimate the amount of time the job will take or wait until the mood strikes), (5) make a daily to-do list, and (6) "dechunk" (which means break tasks into manageable portions with deadlines). Some authorities are more pragmatic: scratch off tasks that you never plan to do; estimate the amount of time you think a job will take and then double it; reward yourself for tasks completed, such as an hour of guilt-free reading.

Uh-oh. That won't work. I already read guilt-free. I also garden, e-mail, nap, and gaze out the window guilt-free. I do recognize that procrastination is part of a larger problem, such as ginning up stress to propel me into a chore. Still, it is nothing I cannot correct.

I scoured the research for milder descriptions that might fit my case: dawdling, stubborn, sensitive to rejection. That is definitely me. I have experienced so much rejection, I have notches on my ego.

I am calmer now. I have a plan of action, and for extra protection, I have discovered a new battery of faux saints for workaday vexations: St. Isidore, patron of computers; St. Vitus, invoked for oversleeping; and, my favorite, St. Expiditus, guardian against procrastination.

I have written a little prayer to St. Expiditus for my condition:

> Let not my will wobble,
> may distractions be faint and few,
> give me self-discipline of steel,
> many thanks and toodily doo.

March 20 or 21 Is the First Day of Spring

Spring Equinox and Deviled Eggs

My friend Jackie says she knows it is spring when old boyfriends start showing up. "They're like trappers," she said, "coming down from the mountains when the snow melts."

Spring does that to us, has us running around as if in a Shakespeare comedy, singing, "Hey, nonny nonny."

The first springlike weekend, my gardening neighbors and I pop out of our homes like gophers. We are armed with rakes and shovels and chain saws. We dig up bushes and move them to new locations. We drag lawn furniture out of the garage. We crop monkey grass until our arms ache.

I dropped by a plant store and was about to plunge headfirst into flowering plants when a seasoned old gent in overalls told me, "Sixty degree weather in Oklahoma in March don't mean nothin'."

I screeched to a halt. He was exactly exact—it *don't* mean nothin'. Gardening too early in Oklahoma is much like those old beaus—one day soon, I'll look outside at the freak frost or late snowstorm of ten or twelve inches and wonder, "What was I thinking?"

And yet, after hibernating all winter, we are starved for color and fresh air.

One spring I inherited a basement office from a woman so morose about her love life that she was as gray as a flounder. Her office had no windows, and she had decorated the cinder-block walls with two big paintings: one was a coiled snake and the other was a green man in a wooden coffin. A couple of days in that place and I would have been depressed, too. I took down the paintings and put up a border of bright paper flowers. Neither the office nor the job worked out, despite my paper flowers and cheery stab at cheap interior decorating.

I need color and light in my life, but a little common sense is good, too. I do not need to make a garden in March and sacrifice it to the elements. There is spring and then there is false spring. Gardening is like the rest of life—a fine line between optimism and lunacy, much like old romances and bad jobs.

So, in false spring, I compromise. I buy a couple of pots of blossoming geraniums, big enough to see but light enough to grab up and rush indoors when the cold threatens to freeze their buds off. I tie colorful ribbons to flutter on the bare tree branches. And I stick a dozen plastic pinwheels in the garden, where they spin like animated jonquils.

I sit outside in the sunny yard all one afternoon, not gardening myself to a froth but sipping mimosas and making a garden plan on paper. Giddy with birdsong and pollen and champagne, I do not give a thought to what lies ahead—Oklahoma summer with equal portions of heat and humidity, insects, and mildew. But neither do I bring out the tender plants from my greenhouse before they are ready to face the world. At dusk, I can look straight up at miles of starlings hurrying to their roosting areas. In this upside-down view, they resemble a school of fish between me and the twilight sky.

I hope Mother Nature is smiling on me and thinking, "She's a slow learner but showing promise."

In March, the sun crosses the celestial equator and stands *en pointe* either March 20 or 21—spring equinox ("equal night"), the first day of spring, when day and night are balanced and the same length.

A couple of days earlier, on the morning of St. Joseph's Day, March 19, the swallows began returning to the San Juan Mission in Capistrano, California. They have done this for centuries, flying fifteen thousand miles, from Goya, in the province of Corrientes in Argentina. They have flown from dawn to sunset, fifteen hours a day, for thirty days. They have had neither food nor water during their urgent flight. That is the force of spring.

Across the continent, every year, a flock of buzzards returns to Hinkley, Ohio, in mid-March. The occasion is marked with a local celebration of far less romance and notoriety than the swallows enjoy. The buzzards seem to have an instinctive memory of a great hunt in the winter of 1818. When the snow melted, the land was littered with dead game and the buzzards came to feed. They have returned ever since. This is spring, too.

We are all of a piece—beaus and buzzards, goofy gardeners and slightly crazed swallows—all hungry for spring.

For some, it is customary to celebrate the first day of spring with eggs, symbols of new life and fertility. Egg dishes, trying to balance a raw egg on end, egg-rolling games, and decorating a hard-boiled egg as a charm are examples. I personally do not know anybody who does any of this, but perhaps these are customs of the more mystical among us, teachers with antsy children to entertain, or people with time on their hands. The closest I have come to this is making deviled eggs for a party.

To celebrate the first day of spring, a group of us planned a salad party. Some were to bring wine, some dessert, and the rest of us were to bring salads. I was a salad.

What I took was cold asparagus and—what proved to be the starring dish—deviled eggs. I became the salad queen. What rhapsodizing, what praise and worship, what exclamations of pure joy resulted—all because of a plate of deviled eggs.

Not that the deviled eggs were particularly good, because they weren't. And not because they were unique, because they weren't that, either. It is because they were plain, simple, old-fashioned deviled eggs. The way my mother used to make them for children's parties.

I am amazed to see how many recipes there are for deviled eggs. The yolk stuffing can be mixed with a jaw-dropping variety of ingredients: capers, olives, pickle relish, curry, shrimp, bacon, guacamole, soy sauce, whipped cream, yogurt, chili powder, jalapeños, and even the Greek liqueur ouzo. They can be topped with caviar.

I suppose this is because the term "deviled" means dark (as in devil's food cake) or highly seasoned (as in deviled ham). Spicy (as in hot as Hades) and anything hot are associated with the devil.

The classic recipe is egg yolk with mayonnaise and mustard powder. But that is too tame for me. I use plain mustard. Sometimes a dash of spicy mustard if I am feeling madcap, but usually plain old French's mustard, salt, and pepper.

For the salad party, I stirred in the tiniest bit of chopped chives and parsley from my herb garden, but mostly these were for color because I didn't have paprika to sprinkle on top.

Oprah Winfrey's favorite deviled egg recipe calls for mayonnaise, mustard, sweet pickle, Worcestershire sauce, lemon juice, horseradish sauce, Tabasco sauce, and parsley. Holy Moly. That is not a deviled egg, that is an occasion.

Stuffed eggs are a main character in *Being Dead Is No Excuse: The Official Southern Ladies Guide to Hosting the Perfect Funeral* by Gayden Metcalfe and Charlotte Hays. "Whenever someone dies in the [Mississippi] Delta," the book says, "you just automatically take stuffed eggs and a bottle of wine. Unless you're Methodist, and then you just take the eggs."

I think the reason my deviled eggs were such a hit is that they are nostalgic and a food from our childhood. They remind us of picnics and parties and holidays and summer. One source called deviled eggs "hors d'oeuvres of the past"—very 1950s.

Heady with my cooking success and moderately crazed for information about deviled eggs, I did some research and found that the recorded history of deviled eggs stretches back to ancient Rome. The oldest recipe for stuffed eggs was in a fifteenth-century Italian cookbook. Stuffed eggs were first named deviled eggs in Great Britain in the eighteenth century.

There is even a National Deviled Egg Day—November 1.

And corny jokes. Here's one. What did the evil chicken lay? Deviled eggs.

Oprah Winfrey's Deviled Eggs

12 large eggs
3 tablespoons mayonnaise
2 tablespoons mustard
1 tablespoon minced sweet pickles
1 dash Worcestershire sauce
salt and fresh ground pepper
1 dash lemon juice
1 dash horseradish
1–2 dashes Tabasco
2 tablespoons chopped parsley
2 tablespoons paprika

Hard boil eggs. Cut each in half lengthwise. Remove yolks and place in bowl with all other ingredients. Mix well. Spoon into egg whites and sprinkle with parsley and paprika. Cover and refrigerate at least one hour or more. Serve chilled.

—From recipezaar.com.

March 30 Is I Am In Control Day

Askgeorge.com

"I'm feeling a little better," I told my ex-husband, Jay.

"Better? I didn't know anything was wrong with you," he said.

"Yes, my hairdresser diagnosed it. I haven't been sick exactly, just sluggish. And something wrong with my stomach." Laboriously, I itemized the symptoms. "Plus, I was puffy. He says it's probably a yeast imbalance that started when I took some antibiotics. Absolutely no sugar, alcohol, or bread for two weeks, he said, and he recommended a soothing drink of sliced cucumber in water with parsley. It's also a diuretic, which should help with the puffiness. Most of all he recommended Multidophilus, which I took, and I'm feeling better already."

"Wait a minute," Jay said. "Go back to that first part. Who diagnosed this?"

"My hairdresser. George."

Silence fell like a dark night.

I love the Information Age. Within two blocks of my house are a university library, a mega-bookstore, a quality used bookstore, and a premium magazine shop. With my computer, I am wired to the Internet and endless facts. I could ask questions and search out answers until the cows come in. With all this information quivering before me like Elysian fields, I should feel in control of my life.

Still.

It is nice to be able to go to one source, one wise person who knows it all. That used to be my mother. Sometimes it is Peter, a knowledgeable Realtor who single-handedly keeps this city going. Peter knows everything about everybody, and he has the top list of repairmen, contractors, carpenters, and attorneys. Mostly, though, it is George, my hairdresser, whom I turn to for advice.

George knows why my zinnias did not germinate, what kind of body work I need for the catch in my back, and how to make nourishing protein cookies for long airplane flights. He has directed me to the health food store to get a fizzy drink to energize me when I have that little sinking spell at five o'clock. He knows how many calories are in all kinds of alcohol. He showed me a great stretch to relieve the tightness between my shoulder blades. He knows the best place in town to buy tennis shoes. He told me how to cook a potent lentil soup and how to keep slugs out of my garden. He explained how to build a tall trellis for morning glories. George knows all the hottest bands, the funniest comedians, and the newest movies. He knows where to buy the naughtiest greeting cards and has quoted most of them to prove it. He has offered to show me the riverbank in Cherokee County with the greatest healing energy, which originates, of course, from a strong magnetic field in the earth.

This font of information comes free with a masterful cut, color, and blow-dry. He was quite cross when I was photographed outside on a windy day without consulting him. My hair was puffed up and sideways like a bad soufflé. He tossed aside the picture in scorn. "I could have done barrel curls that would stand up to gale force winds," he said. "Hurricane Camille could have blown through, but your hair would not have moved."

Naturally George would know that Hurricane Camille, a 1969 Category Five storm, is one of the strongest hurricanes in recorded history.

I am sure there is much more that George could tell me, but he doesn't like to push. In no time at all, he showed me how to do my makeup like Marilyn Monroe. If I want him to, he will teach me how to play African drums and weld.

He has been preoccupied lately, though, with all the homosexual brouhaha from the Baptists and the Catholics and the Episcopalians. George, who is also a musician, is writing a country-western song-commentary about it. The song is titled, "I Been Whupped by the Bible Belt."

April

Modest, let us walk among it,
  With our faces veiled—
  As they say polite Archangels
  Do in meeting God!

  —Emily Dickinson, from poem 65

Baseball Season Begins

Rhubarb

Hot diggedy dog, it's rhubarb season.

And in more ways than one.

Since rhubarb is most popular as a dessert, we think of it as a fruit, but it is actually a vegetable. Those luscious red stalks, begging to be stewed into compotes or pies, can now be found in the grocery store. Such availability was not always the case.

Popularizing rhubarb was a challenge because the leaves are poisonous. Makes sense that it's difficult to get people to eat plants that kill them. The stalk is what is edible—big red stalks that look like celery. But unlike celery, rhubarb is never eaten raw. It is cooked and sweetened and so frequently made into pies, it is also called the "pie plant."

As a dessert, rhubarb is often mixed with apples or strawberries. I prefer it plain—delicious tart rhubarb in a sweet syrup. Maybe with a daub of yogurt. As a sauce, rhubarb is especially good with chicken or salmon.

Rhubarb loves cold climates and was discovered by a naturalist traveling across Siberia in the 1700s. He sent some plants to North America, where it became popular as one of the early plants in the spring garden. "It is the first green thing we see in the garden after a long winter," my friend Hilary said of her Nova Scotia home.

Rhubarb became generally associated with digestive spring-cleaning and was considered a sort of tonic to cleanse the system. The oxalic acid in rhubarb stems makes it useful for scouring cooking pots.

Somewhere along the line, "rhubarb" came into the slang vocabulary, first in Shakespeare's theatre, in which a rhubarb meant a quarrel or meaningless chatter. Then, in the 1940s, it was adopted by American baseball; a "rhubarb" is a stew or a ruckus with the umpires or among players. The broadcaster Red Barber and sportswriter Tom Meany often talked about a rhubarb, especially at home plate. Red Barber even titled his autobiography *Rhubarb in the Catbird Seat*. He called Ebbets Field "the rhubarb patch" because the Brooklyn players seemed to love arguing with the umpires.

Now the au courant thing among young club goers is a drink of the season, and the *New York Times* ran a recipe for a drink of the spring— rhubarb cosmopolitan made with vodka, triple sec, lime juice, and fresh rhubarb juice. Somewhere I came across a recipe for frozen rhubarb daiquiris.

Rhubarb's time seems like a short season: early spring, when baseball games are starting and rhubarb is on the market. Whether we like it in drinks, in pies, in the kitchen scrubbing pots and pans, or on the baseball field, like the red-bosomed robin, rhubarb is a welcome vanguard of spring.

No wonder Garrison Keillor sings, "Be bob a ree bop, rhubarb pie."

Hilary's Rhubarb Crisp Non-recipe

Hilary says: I don't have a recipe.

I mix flour, oats, and brown sugar in a bowl. Then I work in butter with my fingers, and sometimes I add cinnamon. I put that on top of rhubarb cut into half-inch pieces and tossed with sugar. I bake it about 45 minutes in a 350-degree oven.

Daylight Saving Time Begins
the First Sunday in April

Daylight Saving Time

I despise daylight saving time. And I despise Red Statum, the man who is personally responsible for daylight saving time. Actually, I am partially responsible, but Red Statum is the man who talked me into it.

In the 1970s, I was working at a television station and Red was a cameraman in the newsroom. One day he came to me to sign a petition to adopt daylight saving time. In the 1970s, I did not have two thoughts rattling around in my blonde head. As Red explained it to me, this was a great idea because it would give his softball team more time to play after work. That sounded like a valid reason to me, so I signed the petition.

What I did not realize at the time—and, oh, how many tales of woe in my life begin with that phrase—is that this would be with me forever. Until the end of time. Which comes in October when we roll back the clocks, it gets dark about 4:00 in the afternoon, and the sun does not come up until midmorning. Daylight saving time begins at 2:00 A.M. the first Sunday in April, when I begin losing an hour's sleep.

I hate the name "daylight saving time" because it is hard to say. That's why most of us say "daylight savings time." I hate having to fiddle with all my clocks twice a year. I hate the weak rationale, "But in the fall you get an extra hour's sleep." I hate everything about it. My sister lives in Arizona, one of the places that largely does not adhere to daylight saving time, so I can never figure out what time it is there. If I were to call people in Hawaii, American Samoa, Puerto Rico, the Virgin Islands, Guam, and parts of Indiana, I would have the same problem; they don't recognize daylight saving time either. However, if I call someone on the

Navajo Reservation in Arizona, we would be on the same wavelength. I wish I knew somebody there to call. My sister vexes me by lying about the time change.

"It is nine o'clock here," I will say to her. "Straight-up nine. What time is it there?"

"Fifteen after seven," she answers.

Until I did some research, I did not realize that we did not have a standard time in the United States and Canada until 1883 and we did not have time zones in the states until 1918. Then, during World War I, an Englishman came up with the idea of changing the clocks to conserve energy. Same thing during World War II, when it was a national war effort. After the war, however, daylight saving time was the option of state and local communities until 1966. In the 1970s, people began agitating for it, saying it would make transportation, communication, and interstate commerce more uniform. It also saves electrical energy, advocates proclaim.

About this time, Red Statum and his softball team got into the act. Finally, President Nixon signed the daylight saving time Energy Act of 1973, and it became law the following year.

Time has become a looming issue in my life. I never seem to have enough time. It takes more time to do less than ever before. It takes me longer to do anything. "Where does the time go?" I wail to friends, and they answer, "We used to be able to stay awake at night."

Where does the time go? And where does stuff come from? A few years ago I made a vow to walk on more rooftops—be more daring, take more chances, live on the edge. And I am, in a fashion. I find myself living on the edge of my shelves. Everything I eat, use, and apply teeters on the very edge of shelves. I have no idea what is crammed in behind. The medicine cabinet is so full, bottles fall into the sink when it is full of water. Kitchen cabinets are so crammed, vitamin pills with loose lids topple into the dog's dish. Closets, file cabinets, every drawer in the house are all bulging with stuff. It is a daily battle to wrestle clothes out of the closet, where the hangers cling together like orphans in a silent movie. My life is the cosmopolitan version of the forest primeval reclaiming the land. Stuff and daylight saving time have become the menacing, advancing undergrowth that is engulfing my life.

Just as spring is peeping timidly around the corner, daylight saving time hits and it is summer. I am barely acclimated to the time change when daylight saving time is yanked away by some malevolent clock magician. One day it is August and I am lolling around in a lawn chair, the next day it is October and I am running for my life with the holidays hard on my heels. Labor Day, then bang! Autumn is off and running at the speed of a dog race—the frantic start of school and football games and ballet and concerts and then Thanksgiving and Christmas and more stuff!

I hate daylight saving time. Red Statum, wherever he is, better be playing a lot of softball.

April 4 Is Tell a Lie Day

Ex-husbands Patented

Forget Madam Curie. Forget John Nash. Forget Einstein. I am the genius of the era. I have made a discovery that outshines the double helix, the Northwest Passage, and penicillin.

But let me begin at the beginning. Usually I am good at either honoring my commitments or saying "No" up front. "No, I can't go. No, I can't do it. No thank you." But, I don't know, maybe rambunctious spring got to me, and I looked up to discover that I had committed myself to several things I did not want to do.

No reason. I wasn't sick. I had not double-booked myself. I didn't forget. It is just that my choice of Deadly Sin of the Day was sloth. I just did not want to

- Go to the peace rally.
- Drop by the reception.
- Attend the meeting.

No reason at all. I just wanted to stay home, wear baggy clothes, drink coffee, and read. I wanted to sit sideways in my big green chair and drop newspapers on the floor as if a maid would be along later to tidy up.

But. I had told people I would attend, and these were incidents in which the truth would not only make me appear churlish but also would be hurtful and diminishing to the people who had asked me.

What I needed was a great excuse. Not just a good alibi—a great, outrageous, unquestionable excuse.

And that is when I made my discovery. Who could I call to come up with a world-class lie? Who could come up with an alibi so fantastic that it could not even be challenged? A retort that would leave the listener slack-jawed in amazement? The answer was, my ex-husband.

Nobody can tell whoppers like my ex-husband. When it comes to questions that begin with "Where were you . . ." and "Why didn't you . . ." he is gold-medal material. Here is a simple example. After we had both quit smoking with vows and pledges never to smoke again, I came upon him with a cigarette in his hand. "What are you doing?" I asked. He dropped the cigarette in the ashtray and said, quick as a whip, "I was just holding this for a guy."

So I called my ex-husband.

"Jay," I said, "you've got to help me. I need some award-winning excuses for things I didn't do."

"Be happy to," he said, always the congenial chap. "But I can't talk right now. I'm on the other line with the Department of Hazard Removal. I'll call you right back." He didn't.

See what I mean?

Who could hear an excuse like that and say, "Liar, liar, pants on fire?"

Neither could he talk the next morning when I called him again. He had to help a hysterical, elderly neighbor get a family of raccoons out of her attic. And that afternoon, when I called him at work, his office was being evacuated by the bomb squad.

"I'm coming over to your house," I told him finally.

"Great," he said. "Love to see you. But can you bring me some soup and ginger ale because I've broken out in some kind of oozing rash, my eyes are swelling shut, and I have raging diarrhea and vomiting. The doctor says it's fifty-fifty that it's highly contagious."

I did not fall for that. I am not the gullible chump I used to be. I have wised up and learned a few things in my life. I have memorized the Noel Coward lyric: "How could you believe me / When I told you that I loved you / When you know I've been a liar all my life."

What I did was leave the soup and ginger ale on his front porch.

April Is the Month of Aphrodite

A Passion for Bakelite

"Aren't you a Madonna collector?" my friend Glenda began the phone conversation.

"The singer?" says I, often a step or two behind.

The pause was so long I thought the phone was out of order.

"Nooo," she said. "The religious Madonna. Little statues of the Virgin Mary. Do you collect them?"

"I don't think so," I said. My passions and obsessions flip on and off like a light switch, so for all I know, maybe I do collect them. For a couple of years, I was crazy about needlepoint. I made needlepoint pillows until they stacked up like summer clouds. Then, one evening when company was arriving, I kicked my current needlepoint project under the sofa and forgot it. Three months elapsed before I discovered it, and when I did, I looked at it with all the astonishment of making an archaeological discovery. That was the end of my needlepoint phase.

I have also moved through impassioned collections of pressed-glass spooners, wooden folk art, handmade quilts, and cat objects. But when Glenda called, I was in a dry spell, a collection just waiting to happen.

So I went to the estate sale she'd called to tell me about, and I fell in love with the Madonnas. As I went out the door carrying a box of them, I chirped to someone, "And I didn't even know I collected them!" The Madonnas were all over my office, lining every window ledge, until my kitten Veronica began knocking them off, one by one. Clearly a pagan, the kitten left a trail of beheaded Madonnas in her wake until I rescued what was left and relocated them. With cats, I need more durable collectables.

I learned a reverence for garage and estate sales after my mother died. Overnight, all of the beloved objects from the family home became merely stuff. After the most precious things had been distributed to family members, the estate sale was just like others I go to—tables full of trinkets that people pawed through, saying, "I wouldn't give a quarter for this." It was just shabby stuff to them, but to me, every item had a memory.

Some people cannot abide the idea of buying used things, but I love the idea of extending the life of embroidered pillowcases, quaint tea towels, and vintage dishware. I especially love estate sales of glamorous women who decorated their homes and themselves in the fashion of the 1950s. Tiny cut-glass ashtrays used at bridge parties, Oriental home accessories—whenever I take away one of these treasures, I feel as if I am buying a little piece of those women's glamour. I put a stem of orchids in an art deco vase and hope I am carrying their image forward.

I am often inspired to new passions. Last weekend, I fell in love with a white cashmere swing coat from the 1950s or 1960s. And on the way out the door I spied—oh glory, something new to me—Bakelite jewelry. Until that moment, I had never given Bakelite a second glance. That revolutionary plastic, popular from 1920 to 1940, is usually spinach green, butterscotch, yellow, or black. The deeply etched Bakelite pins or bangle bracelets are pricey. Earrings are less expensive. Button shaped or square, they are a touch of hard-time elegance.

It was love at first sight, Bakelite and me. I am not alone. Andy Warhol amassed one of the best collections of Bakelite jewelry in the world.

Wait until you see me in my vintage, white swing coat with three-quarter-length sleeves and my pea-green Bakelite earrings. I am a swirl of memory and bygone elegance for under fifty dollars. Bedangled with Bakelite, I am an Estate Sale Aphrodite in April.

April 18–24 Is National Pet ID Week

A Cat's Life

My cat Lola is a climber. The first time I let her out of the house, she scampered up onto the roof of the house and scaled the chimney. There she stood, a small tabby cat on the tallest point of the property. Passersby stopped their car and took photos of her with head back breathing the fresh air and tail straight up like an antenna. And of me on the ground, hopping from one foot to another like Rumpelstiltskin crying, "Oh. My. God."

Since then Lola has been up on several roofs—mine, the neighbor's, the garage, and up into countless trees. She is such a high-wire act that her son William assumed he had inherited the climbing gene. Nope, it must have skipped a litter. On one of his first ventures outdoors, William got stuck in a pear tree and I had to fetch a ladder to get him down. It was such a traumatic experience that William went back inside and let it be known that if anyone wanted him, they could find him on the kitchen counter. Other cats may scale Mount Everest if they choose; William will watch out the window and nibble tuna treats.

I admire this self-knowledge in my cats. They know what they like and they stick to it. They are not pressured toward self-improvement. They leave that to people. No one tells them to walk an extra mile a day or to learn another language. No new recipes for them. Give my cats a tried-and-true can of fish and let some other cat sample the sautéed veal simmered in gravy.

My cats' motto is this: If you are already happy, why try to be happier? Or the happiest? Life isn't a contest when you are a cat. Those that want to stay inside and sleep on cushions do so. Those that want to go out to the garden go out—and in and out and in. That is practically all the choice they want.

The single objective of every cat that has crossed my threshold—and now by the big yellow dog that lives with us—is to sleep on the Big Bed. No matter how or where they lived before, despite whatever wretched conditions, even if this is the first time they have set foot inside a home, they all have the same reaction when they spot the Big Bed. They stop in their tracks with their eyes glued on this quilt-covered paradise and think, in cat language, "Holy Moly, I have discovered Nirvana."

From that point, they are single minded in gaining access to this homey paradise. The dog is content to steal a surreptitious afternoon nap. The cats manipulate an elaborate caste system, from the exalted pillow beside me to a small corner at the foot of the bed. Whatever space they stake out, they do not rest until they have achieved it. Some cats are fiercely territorial, proclaiming themselves lion king of the mountain. Others are sly and cunning. These are the cats that creep into the bedroom in the middle of the night as softly as a breeze. I awake to find them packed alongside me like sandbags or draped around my head like a wool cap with the earflaps down. Some choose to be treetop cats and some to be countertop cats, but all want to curl up on the Big Bed. They smile in their sleep and dream of singing "Gimme a pig's foot and a bottle of beer."

Cats are creatures that know how to lick life right in the face. I could learn a thing or two from them. If they put it into words, they would say that most humans make a job of being happy. Or that we don't know happiness when we have it. It is easier for a cat. When you are a cat with a safe home and all the freedom you choose, every day is like a whole new Saturday you have never seen before.

April 22 Is Oklahoma Day

Lee Wiley

I grew up during the 1950s and 1960s, when the chic women we saw in magazines and movies were in Manhattan wearing slim black dresses, furs, and picture hats. That image became my hallmark of beauty. In my fantasies, I imagined myself in a New York club sipping drinks in stemmed glasses. I *was Breakfast at Tiffany's*—also luncheon and midnight supper at Tiffany's, in long gloves and lots of eye makeup.

I have just discovered a singer who sings like that image. Ironically, she is from a small Oklahoma town. Before a friend gave me a CD of Lee Wiley, I had not heard of her, but I immediately joined the Lee Wiley cult and began reading about her, researching her, and buying her CDs. She was enormously popular in the 1930s and 1940s and an influence on Billie Holiday and Peggy Lee. She has been inducted into the Oklahoma Jazz Hall of Fame, but she was as popular as a café society singer as a jazz singer. She did not belt out her music—she projected a blend of fragility, vulnerability, sophistication, and sensuality, but she was no cream puff.

Lee Wiley was born in Fort Gibson, Oklahoma, about 1910, but by the time she was in her twenties, she was singing in New York. She was part Cherokee but looked more like Grace Kelly—a cool, elegant blonde with a voice that ranged from warm honey to chilled champagne.

Lee Wiley made her first recording in 1931 as the featured vocalist with Leo Reiseman's band. She went on to perform with Eddie Condon, Benny Goodman, Fats Waller, Paul Whiteman, and the Dorsey brothers. For a while in the 1940s, she was married to jazz pianist Jess Stacy and toured with his band. Some say it was her spendthrift habit that destroyed the band. Her career was full of bumps, and her biography is full of mystery. She may have had medical problems, tuberculosis, and temporary blindness that forced her to take time off to recuperate. She may have fought with producers who bounced her off a radio program. Hers was a life with spice.

She sang the works of early-twentieth-century composers: George Gershwin, Richard Rodgers and Lorenz Hart, Cole Porter, and Harold Arlen. She was the first singer to record an album of a single composer in what is now the familiar "songbook" format. For jazz fans, her best albums are *Night in Manhattan* and *West of the Moon,* both recorded in the 1950s.

Lee Wiley has been called a "femme fatale of jazz" and a "chantoosy" —one of the white goddesses of the big band era. Until 1929, only male vocalists were featured with bands. She was one of the first and perhaps the greatest of the girl singers. Her peers were Connee Boswell and Mildred Bailey. After them came Billie Holiday, Peggy Lee, Kay Starr, Lena Horne, Rosemary Clooney.

One music historian wrote about seeing Lee Wiley in New York for the first time. It was at the Art Deco club. She was a beautiful woman swathed in furs, accompanied by four men in white tie and tails. They sat around her in a banquette, lit her cigarettes, laughed at her witticism, and ignored the piano player, Bobby Short.

She had a voice, a music critic said, like a sheer negligee.

She died in 1975. For several decades before that, her talent glittered and dazzled New York. It still does on records and CDs—Lee Wiley, Indian, glamorous girl singer from Oklahoma.

April Is National Gardening Month

Late Bloomer

Nroom!

Did you hear that? That sound like the Indy 500? That was spring roaring through.

April is National Gardening Month, but some years in Oklahoma it does not hang around to celebrate.

Whenever we have one of those years, by early April, the daffodils are only memories of yellow. The redbuds have already passed from purple blossoms to green leafiness and the tulips are singing the Patsy Cline ballad "I Fall to Pieces." The early spring color that bursts upon us with rambunctious promise has hurried through, on to a rendezvous elsewhere.

Most Aprils, hedges of brilliant azaleas reign yet, alongside lacy white spirea. Dainty columbine teeters in the wind beside the low knobs of herbs that seem to appear out of nowhere, full of health and promising a long summer. I wish I had planted lettuce back in February. I could be eating salad from my garden now.

Is it only in fiction that four seasons share the year as neatly as a pie cut in four pieces? Only in movies that one season gives way politely to another, sharing the stage like four gracious dancers, each leaving with a curtsy and a bow? Do the four seasons exist distinct and separate only in Vivaldi's music? Because in real life—or in Oklahoma, which is as real and alive as it gets—the seasons elbow and shove one another like rascally schoolchildren in a photograph.

Everywhere, I find time, past and present, blurring together.

In South Africa, I had trouble sleeping. Twice I had nightmares that a rapist was in my room. Once I dreamed that my wrists were bound. Many times, half asleep, I longed for my mother. When I told my South

African hosts of these heart-pounding dreams, they nodded and said, "We have those dreams, too. The spirits are strong here. South Africa is a world of extremes, and the spirits slip in through the cracks." It is a country of extremes—privilege or poverty, beautiful and bountiful or barren, lush vineyards and unpaved homelands, men in white playing cricket and barefoot women carrying pails of water on their heads.

Another South African told me, "Troubled spirits still move across this land. Remember," he said, "that J.R.R. Tolkien was born here. Think of this as the setting for his books." True or not, when I thought of South Africa as the landscape for hobbits and wizards—of shires and downs, of mirkwood forests and dark shadows—I understood the land better.

Jean Thomas was an old woman and my spiritual mentor when she told me about her spiritual trip to Iona, a tiny island off the coast of Scotland known as a sacred place. In the year 563, St. Columbia stepped ashore there and began converting Scotland to Christianity. The miracle of Iona, according to the travel-guide literature, is that in barbarian wilderness, Iona became "the center for this world and the next." Sages went there for wisdom, kings for consecration and confession. "It's a thin place you're going," a Scotsman told her as the boat left shore, "so hold fast to your soul."

On some of Oklahoma's prairies, in Osage County especially, I often feel the spirit of my father as a rowdy young cowboy. Invincible, cocky, a young daredevil not yet into World War II and the paratroopers. A young man in a young state, as free and restless as the raw prairie winds. If the light is right, a past I did not know slips in close to my face.

When I was a young adult, my father was appalled to learn that I was taking horseback riding lessons. "You're paying someone to teach you to ride a horse," he said. "My God, you've been riding horses all your life." "No, Dad," I said. "*You* have been riding horses all my life."

I had trouble learning to ride, trouble being adventurous enough. Once, my regular teacher wasn't there and the stable's owner filled in. She was an older woman, as tanned and tough as a boot. That summer's evening I was trying yet again to canter, but instead I was bouncing along in a rough trot like a greenhorn. She watched me in disgust and said, "As many lessons as you've had, you ought to get it by now."

People say that to me a lot. A beautician once told me, "As much as we've done for you, you ought to look better than you do."

I agree. I wish I were better. Faster. Earlier.

I ought to run a classified ad: "Wanted—one lesson learned the easy way."

I wish I had written that line myself instead of stealing it.

Perhaps I am a late bloomer, like the lilacs and peonies that hover just now on the edge of a mighty profusion. Like long summer days rousing themselves to head this way. Like South Africa, creating a new democracy out of a troubled history.

April 22 Is Earth Day

Bumblebee Season

April is bumblebee season at my house. Bumblebees as round as marbles buzz around the wisteria and then—I swear this is true—drill holes with their tails in the wooden arbor. They are miniature tornadoes boring into the wood. What are they doing in there? Laying eggs, I guess. Preparing a hole worthy of a queen, perhaps. Why the arbor and not the fence or windowsill? I cannot fathom the bumblebee heart. I do not even know what species of the *Bombus* genus these are. All I know is that they appear to be bumblebees with a fierce desire for the wisteria arbor, which is starting to look like Swiss cheese.

"You can get insecticide that will drive away the bumblebees," someone told me. "You could seal up the holes with them inside," someone else said. I cannot do either, any more than I can follow the advice to have my cats declawed. I just keep reupholstering the furniture.

I think it is important for us human animals to find our place among the rest of the earth's creatures. They help us keep in touch with the seasons. My cats and dog remind me of the changing seasons by shedding with a vengeance. They drop hair like spoiled children strewing dirty clothes through the house. The more I vacuum, the more I know summer is ending or coming and it is time to change fur.

Human life is so rich, we have several calendars to choose from. Our year starts several times.

For much of my life, the year started in the fall and involved education. From elementary school, as a kid with scuffed brown oxfords and skinned knees, through graduate school and then teaching at a university, my year began with the start of the fall semester and ended with spring graduation. Then I worked for a ballet company and the performing arts season began in the fall. Christmas holiday for others was

Nutcracker season for us. Poker-faced stagehands sometimes wore buttons that read, "Christmas is a Nutcracker."

Time can rotate on the axis of the calendar year or the fiscal year. Gardeners live by the rhythm of the growing season. For sports fans, the seasons span the calendar, culminating with the bowl games in winter, the world series in the fall, and the basketball playoffs in the spring. Some churchgoers can watch the liturgical year change with the shifting colors of the vestments and altar cloths, ranging from the long summer season of green to the passionate purple seasons of Lent and Advent.

My grandmother used to say that we would be okay if we could just make it to wild onion time, which is often April. That meant we had gotten through another winter.

Oklahoma Indians say that when the dogwood blooms, the pow-wow season gears up.

I am not all that far removed from my own animal instinct. I love Mary Oliver's line of poetry: "You only have to let the soft animal of your body love what it loves." On a lower plane, I know that I am in the grip of dark winter when I have a desperate and immediate compulsion to lighten my hair color with products from the drugstore. This has resulted in unfortunate colors from the fruit and vegetable palate: apricot, peach, and even artichoke heart.

Of all the calendars, the commercial season of the secular world is the one that makes me most anxious. The calendar months and the season items on the store shelves are out of sync. By August, the stores are full of Halloween things, and in October the shelves are stuffed with Christmas decorations.

My friend Maridel observes the seasons at the neighborhood bakery. At Eastertide she revels in cupcakes frosted with green coconut. Valentine's Day is full of red cookies. Mardi Gras cakes are decorated in gaudy colors of purple, green, and gold.

A psychologist once espoused the theory that the most isolating invention of our society was air conditioning. We used to sit on the front porch, visit with the neighbors, and fan ourselves with paper fans from funeral homes. Now we go inside, close the doors, turn on the air conditioning, and shut out the world.

There is something to her theory. April is one of the few times of year in Oklahoma that I have my windows open. I do not kid myself that this is fresh air, because I know it is full of mold and pollen, but it is also full of spring sounds. I can hear the world and it doesn't sound like central heat and air. A soft night thickens with chirps and trills and hums and throbs. Birds start stirring before dawn. These are old-fashioned sounds, the sound of the natural earth running its engine on idle.

A workman at my house the other day was sympathetic about my bumblebee problem. He told me that recently, while he was mowing his lake property for the first time of the year, bumblebees started buzzing him. He ducked and swatted and dodged and finally lost his temper, he said, got his shotgun, and started shooting at them.

"You were shooting at bumblebees?" I asked.

"Just for a little while," he said. "Then the sheriff drove up. Said someone reported hearing gunfire. Wanted to know if I'd heard it."

"What did you say?"

"I said, 'Who me? I'm just mowing the grass. First time of the season.'"

Spring will do that to us. After he had gone, I said to my own bumblebees, "I hope you heard that. That's the kind of thing that could happen to you if you keep drilling holes in the arbor."

April Is National Poetry Month

Poetry Burning Bright

I was once a member of a poetry-reading ensemble called the Tyger's Eye. We were a quartet of voices and gave performances to civic groups, professional organizations, public events—anywhere anyone would invite us. We would read at the drop of a hat. Rhymes with "cat."

We liked to spell "Tyger" with a *y.* Rhymes with "sky." We were all associated with a university and thought it seemed more scholarly that way. Rhymes with "pay," although we rarely saw any of that. Our performances were art for art's sake, which meant free.

The Tyger's Eye was founded by Winston Weathers, a William Blake scholar, hence the name of the group—"Tyger tyger, burning bright."

We read all kinds of poetry, but the poems usually assigned to me were those with a simple rhythm and meaning. This is because I was the simplest member of the quartet. Once I read a poem by Pablo Neruda titled "Ode to a Pair of Socks."

During Poetry Month one year, I heard a fragment of a poem by Edna St. Vincent Millay. She's the poet who wrote,

> My candle burns at both ends,
> It will not last the night
> But ah, my foes, and oh, my friends—
> It gives a lovely light.

Edna St. Vincent Millay was a poet of another age. She was born in 1892 and grew up in the seaside town of Camden, Maine. The poem that established her career as a major poet was published when she was only twenty. After graduating from Vassar, she moved to Greenwich

Village, where she became known as a bohemian, a feminist, and a poet. She was a member of the Provincetown Players group, along with Eugene O'Neill. She was enormously popular and considered one of the most important literary personalities in America. The *New York Times Book Review* called her "America's Poet of the Future." In 1923 she became the second poet to receive the Pulitzer Prize. The first, in 1922, was Edward Arlington Robinson. The third, in 1924, the year after Miss Millay, was Robert Frost.

And yet, Edna St. Vincent Millay was not sanctified by the literati, which was mostly male. Some critics considered her work too feminine, too popular, too emotional, and too lyrical. She was writing at a time when poets such as Ezra Pound and T.S. Eliot were introducing a new kind of poetry called "modernism." It was a male-defined movement.

She wrote about nature, love, loss, spiritual rebirth, personal freedom, women's sexuality, and the state of the world. Much of her poetry used traditional literary devices such as assonance ("way" and "bay"), consonance ("stem" and "them"), alliteration (singing sweet songs), and onomatopoeia ("hush" and "shush"). Her poems were so musical that one critic said "they coax the language to sing."

Well, obviously if the Tyger's Eye had read any of her poems they would have been given to simple me. I might have read this short poem titled "Grown Up":

> Was it for this I uttered prayers,
> And sobbed and cursed and kicked the stairs,
> That now, domestic as a plate,
> I should retire at half-past eight?

I like that metaphor—domestic as a plate.

She died in 1950 at the age of fifty-two, and half a century later, her poems are still read. That would have pleased her, because one that she wrote was almost like a cry—"Read me, don't let me die."

A poet today who is better known for her prose than for her poetry is Kathleen Norris, who wrote the best-selling book *The Cloister Walk* and, before that, *Dakota—A Spiritual Geography*. Miss Norris tells about teaching poetry to children. One was a little girl from a nearby reservation from a family so poor that she had no paper at home. So, the little girl said, "I write them in my head until I get to school and then copy them down with a pencil."

Here are a couple of poems from the children—poems as beautiful and direct as an arrow's flight.

One elementary school girl who had just moved to Dakota and was overwhelmed by Big Sky country wrote,

> The sky is full of blue
> And full of the mind of God.

And another wrote,

> When my third snail died
> I said I was through with snails.
> But I didn't mean it.

Once for Valentine's Day I wrote a news feature story with a poetry professor. I asked him this question: Why don't we talk in rhyme all the time?

And he told me that poetry, with its rhythms and vocabulary, is a powerful language that speaks to and from our deepest emotions. So when we want to communicate something beyond words, we speak in poetic language. We use it for rituals and ceremonies, state occasions, church—and love.

I think once poetry is in us, we don't forget it; the fragments are always there.

Without the Tyger's Eye, I hardly ever read poetry aloud these days. But when I got a gray tiger-striped kitten, I named him William Blake.

May

A little Madness in the Spring
Is wholesome even for the King

—Emily Dickinson, from poem 1333

The First Thursday in May Is
the National Day of Prayer

Now, Play Nice

What is it about the human species that it cannot get along in groups? I have never been in any organization that did not eventually come to a great falling out. Arts, social service, animal rescue, education—it does not seem to matter how high a purpose the group was organized to serve. At some point we all break into skirmishes, power plays, backstabbing, malicious rumors, malevolent strategizing, name calling, hair pulling, and what my daddy called "old-fashioned butt kicking." Some people are driven away and some resign in outrage. Sometimes the entire organization suffers or even collapses; other times it pulls itself together and goes on better than ever.

As incredible as this may seem, one of the worst organizational catfights I have seen was at church. You might think that in a sacred setting we would behave better, put our differences aside, adopt beatific expressions, and rise above it while singing hymns of joy. You would be oh so wrong. That did not happen. What did happen was a battle of such passion that it made cockfighting look like the Westminster Kennel Club's dog show.

We were the Inquisition all over again, determined to vanquish the infidel. Wild eyed with self-righteousness, people on both sides of the issue would clench their teeth and fists and declare that this was, by damn, a house of peace and it was going to stay that way. Evenings were filled with hissing phone calls, secret meetings, and rumormongering. Letter-writing campaigns were launched. Facts were stretched like Silly Putty. Half-truths were dressed up prettily and flung through the parish as if they were Mardi Gras candy. Emotional pleas rang out.

Yellow ribbons of support were distributed and worn like poppies on Armistice Day. Eyewitness accounts were repeated second- or third-hand, sometimes embellished with garish detail. Statistics of various kinds were gathered and stacked like cordwood while someone would say, "There's the proof, right there in those numbers." And someone would reply, "The Bible says feed my sheep, not count them." We wielded Scripture like a bludgeon.

Sunday mornings, we fearless gladiators marched resolutely into church, sat with our own clutch of supporters—faces as hard as walnuts, mouths turned down, whispering sotto voce how we despised the rector or the vestry or the bishop—and then turned to one another with bright smiles to pass the peace.

In public forums, advocates of the accursed rector or vestry or bishop would weep in emotional soliloquies referring to the accused as "This man of God" or "This selfless paragon of Christianity" while their opposition sat with crossed arms and scornful faces as fixed as a skillet. People stormed out, rose in protest, and circulated petitions.

The peace seekers who chose to avoid the fray and stay at home were dragged into the battle in absentia. Their very absence was ammunition for the attending faithful, who would blame one another: "Look at these empty seats. You are driving people away. You are killing this house of worship."

"Not me," a stalwart Christian would declare. "I was here before the [rector or vestry or bishop (or whoever was being scourged)] and by God I'll be here after he's gone."

There is nothing quite like a sanctimonious skirmish of volunteers in a public place. It was a mercy that no alcohol or weapons were in evidence, but civilized humans can do quite a lot of damage armed only with by-laws, mission statements, seniority, and a righteous sense of duty.

Ah, by-laws and articles of incorporation—these are the things that raise us above the animals. The other animals, I mean. Blessings on us all, creatures great and small.

May Day, Mother's Day,
Cinco de Mayo, Memorial Day

May Days

Ironic, isn't it, that the term "May Day" summons up an image of young couples having picnics on carpets of wildflowers and that it is also the signal for distress by aircraft and ships.

Maybe not so ironic after all, when I remember some of my romances.

May rouses primordial stirrings, perhaps because of its pagan roots. In May, Virgil said, Roman youths went into the fields to dance and sing in honor of the goddess Flora. On the first day of May in 1791, a London newspaper reported that women went into the fields to bathe their faces with dew to make themselves more beautiful. The English celebrated May Day with games and sport, especially archery, a Maypole, and eventually the honorary lord and lady of May known as Robin Hood and Maid Marian.

The Anglo-Saxons called this month *thrimilce* because cows could be milked three times a day. The old Dutch name was Bloumaand ("blossoming month"), and the month's present name probably refers to the Latin name Maia, after the goddess of growth and increase. Yet the month is not just about new life and abundance. More suicides are committed in May than any other month, according to the National Mental Health Association.

May Day

When I was a little girl, we made paper baskets in school for May Day, May 1. They were cut and glued from our Big Chief tablet. On the way home, I filled the basket with little fistfuls of wilting wildflowers. I hung the paper basket on the front doorknob, knocked on the door, and then hid. Year after year, my mother was thrilled to discover this beautiful creation. And so surprised! She never knew it was from me until I jumped out and told her. When I was grown, I took or sent her a basket of flowers every May Day. After she died, I found the enclosure cards tucked into a jewelry box.

Mother's Day

In the United States, the second Sunday in May is Mother's Day. Juliet Ward Howe, author of "The Battle Hymn of the Republic," proposed a Mother's Day in 1870 as a day dedicated to peace. She hoped that the mothers of the world would unite in opposition to war. The holiday was begun in 1907 (some say 1908) by a Philadelphia Sunday school teacher and organist named Anna Jarvis when she persuaded church leaders to hold special church services honoring maternal love. It was the second anniversary of her mother's death, and she wanted carnations (her mother's favorite flower) to become the symbol of love for mothers. Miss Jarvis began to campaign for a national Mother's Day and in 1910, Oklahoma and West Virginia proclaimed the second Sunday in May to be celebrated as Mother's Day. In 1914, President Woodrow Wilson officially proclaimed it a national observance. Carnations may be the official Mother's Day flower, but my grandmother told our family to wear a red rose to honor a living mother and a white rose in memory of a deceased mother.

In England, Mothering Sunday dates from the 1600s, but its origins can likely be traced to ancient spring rituals. On Mothering Sunday (which is traditionally the fourth Sunday of Lent), children of all ages visited their mothers. Servants were given the day off to see their mothers. Children took a simnel cake (or mothering cake) as a gift. The cake's name derived from *simila,* the Latin term for its ingredient of high-quality flour. In return, mothers dispensed a special blessing. Workers walking along country lanes—gone "a-mothering," it was said—gathered wildflowers, which they fashioned into nosegays for their mothers, and this supposedly began the custom of sending flowers for Mother's Day. By the nineteenth century, Mothering Day had become an established holiday when families gathered to attend church together, enjoy a big meal of roast veal or lamb afterward, and treat the mother of the family like royalty.

Cinco de Mayo

May 5 is Cinco de Mayo, a Mexican holiday celebrating the Mexican soldiers' victory over the French army in 1862. It is celebrated more and more in Oklahoma as our state's Hispanic population grows. A local art gallery has a Cinco de Mayo art sale that features paintings by artists fledgling and famous. The paintings are all on 5" × 5" canvas, and they all sell for $50. The gallery opens at 5 minutes until 5 P.M., May 5. What a stampede to get inside.

Although my grandfather's name was Louis Andrea Don Carlos and he spoke Spanish with his brother—or, my cynical Aunt Ila says, they just made up words to make us think it was Spanish—and although my mother went around the house singing "Cielito Linda," I never paid much attention to my Spanish heritage until I acquired a Hispanic brother-in-law. The first time I met Franke Romero, he and my sister, Candee, flew in from Tucson and cooked a Mexican feast for Thanksgiving dinner—*carnitas* and Spanish rice and refried beans (authentically thinned with a little milk).

Memorial Day

Memorial Day is a May holiday we called Decoration Day in my family. It was a time to clean and decorate graves. Memorial Day became an official holiday in 1971, but it began in the mid-1800s with the tradition of honoring the soldiers who died in the Civil War. The date May 30 was chosen, according to legend, because that was the day Napoleon's remains were returned to France from St. Helena. In time, Memorial Day became a day to honor not only those who died in battle, but also all the friends and family whom we want to remember.

In her memoirs, Agnes de Mille wrote about summers starting with Memorial Day, when families who could afford to do so left the hot city to live in the country and returned only at Labor Day. It's nice to think of summer closed in by those holidays, like parentheses.

According to Joyce Sequechie Hifler's *Cherokee Feast of Days,* May is "planting month," which ends with the Green Corn Festival. Almanacs and tradition give the full moons many names. The full moon of May is also known as Flower Moon, Hare Moon, or the Milk Moon. May is a time of green garden plenty—fresh chives and parsley, early lettuce, green beans, and peas, all hurtling toward the summer's end with zucchini and tomatoes up to our ears. But in May, the hard work of autumn's harvest is far away.

Summer's end used to be even more distant. Childhood summers were much longer than they are now. In small-town Oklahoma, summers were times for taking vacations to Grand Lake with water skiing or all-night fishing trips to Moon Lake with smelly dough bait, seining minnows from the Verdigris River, consuming backyard feasts of chilled watermelon and homemade ice cream, roasting wieners and marshmallows on inky nights, and, during the merciless afternoon, hanging motionless in the tire swing trying to remember what a breeze was, so hot and so bored that I could not breathe. Now I think of the month as gentle May, a time to downshift from busy workweek winter. Roses cascade over the picket fence, the grass is cool and damp. Clouds pile up like drop biscuits.

This May Day I will put flowers on my mother's grave, then settle in for the long, green summer. May is one of the best months for gardening in Oklahoma. Peonies, irises, and clematis all vie for attention. Since May is one of the rainiest months in Oklahoma, the hydrangeas bud and blossom happily. The artists of the annual downtown Mayfest greet the rain with less cheer. (The second rainiest month is October, the month of our other outdoors festival, Octoberfest.) Unless it is too cool and rainy, hollyhocks begin to bloom in May. Azaleas have already faded, and it is time to prune and fertilize them. The temperatures where I live average in the upper 70s in the day and mid-50s at night.

May afternoons are sweet when I can sit in dappled sunshine with a book, mint from my garden floating in iced tea, and a garden cat sleeping in the shade. Summer will toughen and show its teeth, but for now, the heat of summer is still a lifetime away. Labor Day is forever away. It is May and, for now, summer is as tender as the start of a romance.

Simnel Cake

> 1½ cups butter
> 4 cups sugar
> 4 cups flour
> ⅓ cup grated lemon and orange peel
> 8 eggs
> 2 cups currants
> 1 teaspoon salt
> 8 ounces or more of almond paste

Cream together butter and sugar. Add eggs, beating after each one. Sift and add flour and salt. Dust peel and currants with flour and add to batter. Line 12" × 15" greased pan with wax paper. Pour in half the batter. Roll out the almond paste and put on top of batter. Top with remaining batter. Bake at 300 degrees for approximately one hour. May be iced. Cut the rich cake into 1" squares.

—From *The Christina Year: A Cookbook for Holy Days and Seasons,*
by the Women of St. Thomas of Canterbury,
Anglican Catholic Church, Roanoke, Virginia.

A good frosting is ⅔ cup softened butter beaten until light; 3 ½ cups confectioners' sugar beaten into the batter until the mixture is fluffy; 2 teaspoons vanilla and 3 tablespoons (or a bit more) milk added and beaten until smooth.

Candee's Carnitas

3 or 4 thick, boneless pork chops
2 cans salsa verde
Serrano pepper (or similar yellow pepper)
Jalapeño pepper (or any hot green pepper)
Oregano
Salt and pepper
¼ to ½ cup onion
3 cloves garlic
Vegetable oil

In a deep skillet, heat oil to medium hot. Salt, pepper, and dust each pork chop with oregano. Insert a slice of garlic in each pork chop and brown on both sides in hot oil. Reduce heat, add a little water if necessary, cover, and simmer until done.

Remove pork chops and add onion, garlic, and sliced peppers to juice. Simmer on low until tender. Cube pork chops and return to sauce. Add more water if too dry. Add salsa verde to cover pork chops, and heat.

Serve with hot tortillas and hotter Spanish rice.

Serves three or four.

Franke's Spanish Rice

1 cup long-grain rice (uncooked)
½ medium onion, chopped fine
2 cloves of garlic, shaved fine
Salt and pepper
Vegetable oil
1 cup grated cheese (optional)
2 cans pato sauce (green)
1 can tomato sauce
Oregano

Cover bottom of saucepan with ¼ inch of oil and heat to medium.
Stir in uncooked rice until lightly browned. Add onions and garlic
with 1-½ cups water, bring to boil. Stir constantly. Boil for 30 sec-
onds (full boil), continuing to stir. Reduce heat to medium. Add 1
can pato sauce and 1 can tomato sauce, stirring constantly. Pepper
to taste (approximately ½ to 1 teaspoon). Simmer on medium heat.
Add oregano to taste (approximately ½ teaspoon). Check consistency of rice. When soft, add 1 can pato sauce and salt to taste.
Remove from heat and stir in cheese.

Will serve three or four. To reheat later, add a little water.

May Is Older Americans Month

Age Appropriate

When I was in my twenties, I made a vow never to be obsessed with age. And I never was. When I was in my twenties.

When I was in my thirties and speaking at a women's conference, I heard another speaker talk about discrimination. Of all the discrimination she had faced—race, gender, age, or marital status—age discrimination was the worst. "Once people know your age," she said, "they put you in a box and say, 'You're too old for this,' or 'You're old enough to know better than that.'"

She observed that when people talk about their age, it is to boast because they think they look so good. I wasn't very sensible about many things when I was thirty, but that made a lot of sense to me, so I have always avoided advertising my age. People accuse me of being secretive or vain, but I have stuck to my guns and thought, in that loving philosophy one develops with age, "If they don't like it, to hell with them."

Birthdays click by like railroad ties. Just yesterday, it seems, young men would pass me and murmur, "Foxy chick." Now young men approach me in the grocery store and ask, "Pardon me, ma'am, is this a zucchini?" It's not just a gender thing. Young women ask me, "Do you know where the baby food is?" Obviously the appearance I project is a woman of some maturity who knows her way around the grocery store.

I see that age has mellowed me. I have gone from ignoring flirtatious young men, or stabbing them with icy glares, to saying patiently, "No, son, that is a cucumber. This is a zucchini and this is a squash." I am a woman who knows her vegetables.

I do not care for the term "geezer babe," but I notice that when traveling I now pack more vitamins and supplements than beauty aids.

Suddenly all of my doctors look about sixteen. I don't care about their medical certificates; I hope they have drivers' licenses.

I realize with a giddy sense of empowerment that I know some other truths that come with maturity:

- I do not have to pour tea for everyone, because they are not all going to like me anyway and I don't care.
- Being smart and tough is not enough and being open and vulnerable has its rewards.
- I have reached an age of confidence. There are some things I don't feel obliged to ever have to do again. I don't ever have to see another production of *Our Town*. I don't ever have to listen to another song by the Beach Boys.
- I do not have to go to 7 A.M. business meetings.
- I don't have to explain, I don't have to justify, I don't have to make excuses. I can say, "No, I don't want to."

When I was in the fourth grade and a tomboy, what I wanted for my birthday was a jean bag, a denim purse that threaded onto your belt with jeans. This was great for bicycle transportation.

When I was in the sixth grade and going to spring dances, the birthday gift I wanted was a short, white fluffy coat.

This year for my birthday, I bought myself a new mop. And I recognize the gift in being able to say, "No, thank you."

None of these is better than the others. They are all (dare I use this phrase) age appropriate. And they are all wonderful. Happy birthday to us all.

The Second Week of May
Is National Herb Week

Primroses

I do not want to be overly optimistic, but I think I just figured out something I have been pondering for thirty years or so. It is a poem about primroses.

I first read the poem when I was at Coffeyville College in Kansas and a devoted student of J. Henry Hedley's literature class. We were young and passionate about words and literature and writing. And about one another.

Mr. Hedley tried to corral this free-flowing passion into academic productivity and learning. One thing he taught us was the difference between the art and the artists who create it—not to confuse the writer with the writing. At least he tried to teach us this. Many of us were too enamored of art to hear it. We admired Fitzgerald and Hemingway, who drank and partied to their deaths. We were too silly and romantic to understand the desperate griminess of alcoholism, addiction, and early deaths. We could not grasp it because we were holding too tightly to our romantic notions.

Recently a friend of mine—adult, educated, responsible—was wounded by a hurtful remark from an artist. It was a superficial wound (only her feelings were hurt), but my friend is a starry-eyed aficionado of the arts. She adores art and the artists who make it happen: singers, dancers, actors, painters, writers—heavenly creatures all, to her. No matter how many accounts she hears of artists' human behavior, she refuses to believe it. Selfish, narcissistic, rude, demanding? Not her artists. So she suffered mightily from this passing affront.

That is because she was not a student of Mr. Hedley's literature class. Perhaps she did not see the Woody Allen movie *Sweet and Lowdown* with Sean Penn as a vain, selfish artist. Or the older movie *A Face in the Crowd* starring Andy Griffith. Or the James Thurber short story about a gifted artist with a nasty disposition.

Hasn't she read about Johann Sebastian Bach, arguably the greatest composer in the history of Western music? Bach the composer was a genius. As for Bach the man, we know little biographical detail. He was a professional musician and an upright middle-class citizen. He was married twice and was the father of twenty children. He was a dutiful cantor in Leipzig and a working musician who did his job: serenade visiting royalty, direct a choir, write a cantata every Sunday. He did it—he wrote more than three hundred cantatas—but he complained constantly about his salary. He was stubborn, had a temper, and was hard to get along with. Once he made such a fuss about a job that he was jailed.

In his day, Bach was not acclaimed as a great composer. He was considered a municipal civil servant hired to oversee the music in four downtown Lutheran churches. Moreover, he was the second choice. His employers in town hall grumbled because their first choice turned them down and they had to make do with Bach, whom they considered mediocre. I hope I remember that the next time I feel hard done by and unappreciated.

I'll tell myself: Do not put too much value in other people's opinions. Do not expect too much from people in charge and don't think too much of yourself. Do your job and deliver your cantata like any other working stiff.

Artists make art. Businessmen make money. Cows make milk. Don't expect any more. We can *hope* for honor, honesty, and kindness, but don't expect special behavior from an artist any more than from a cow.

Part of this I learned in Mr. Hedley's classes, and part in a meditation seminar. The Zen message is, However we try to resist, things are as they are.

So, enlightenment! At last I've got it, the meaning of the poem about primroses. And here is that little poem by William Wordsworth:

> A primrose by the river's brim
> A yellow primrose was to him,
> And it was nothing more.

This is in no way meant to diminish the little primrose. It may be small but it is mighty. The primrose has its own day: April 19 is Primrose Day. The second week of May is National Herb Week, and the primrose is classified as an herb. It shares billing with the violet as Flowers of the Month. Such brave little plants.

The primrose is the first blossom of spring. Winter is still prowling around when I rush to the nursery and buy armfuls of brightly colored primroses to plant in a circle around the birdbath, to line the windowsills, to give as favors at parties. Purple, pink, fuchsia, yellow, and lavender—primroses are spring happiness in small pots. If promises came in color, they would be primroses.

Besides gladdening our spirits, for centuries the multipurpose primrose has been used in cosmetics, jam, and wine. An antique pottage recipe called for rice, almonds, honey, saffron, and ground primrose flowers. Primrose leaves can be eaten in a salad. Pliny the Elder, John Gerard, and Nicholas Culpeper—a trio of long-ago naturalists/herbalists/physicians—praised the primrose's healing qualities as an emetic, astringent, and sedative. The plant (flower, leaf, and root) was used medicinally for muscle aches, to heal wounds, and to treat gout, coughing, insomnia, headache, nervousness, and hysteria. Gerard said, "Primrose Tea drunk in the month of May is famous for curing the phrensie."

Gimme it! A pretty little primrose, modest and useful, to soothe my beastly qualities while I am hammering out my own workaday versions of Bach cantatas.

I may replenish my little herb garden in May, but it is fall when I cut great hands full and steep them in champagne or rice vinegar to make herbal vinegar. I bottle and seal this vinegar to use myself and to give as gifts. For gift bottles, I affix the following tag. (Note: I don't use all of the herbs listed in every concoction, and usually I just use one or two.)

Connie & Herb
Herb Champagne Vinegar

Flavored with herbs from my garden—chives, lemon balm,
parsley, savory, thyme, marjoram, oregano, tarragon.
Nutritious, delicious, medicinal.

Folklore says these herbs: impart courage, dispel melancholy, enhance passion, protect against witchcraft, develop vigor, make men and women glad and merry, and enable one to see the Fairies.

Herbal Vinaigrette

¾ cup olive oil (or salad oil)
¼ cup herb-flavored vinegar
½ teaspoon salt
¼ teaspoon pepper

Blend all ingredients. Shaking them in a jar with a lid is the easiest way. Makes 1 cup.

Use as a salad dressing. Drizzle over vegetables (cold asparagus or sliced tomatoes) or on cold pasta, or to add pizzazz to potato salad or egg salad.

May Is National Salad Month

Lists

I was going out the door to give a speech and I had three thoughts:

1. I wish my hair looked better.
2. I wish I had prepared better.
3. I wish I had never agreed to do this.

I had almost the same experience the day I had book club at my house. Moments before my guests arrived, I had three thoughts:

1. I wish my hair looked better.
2. I wish I had started preparations yesterday or got up earlier today.
3. I wish I had never agreed to do this.

Despite my anxiety, the event turned out better than I had expected, until the guests began drifting away. "Hold it," I said. "Nobody move. Nobody leaves this house until somebody goes to the bathroom. Until somebody notices how clean the grout is and that the lime stains around the faucet are gone. Do you people think I cleaned the bathroom for my own amusement?"

Why is it that giving parties is harder than it used to be—takes longer to get ready, costs more, is more stressful? Not everybody feels that way. Some people love to entertain, cook as relaxation, and make cleaning up a social time. Some people pierce their tongues, too, but I am not one of them.

Not that I haven't gone through phases of hosting dinner parties, teas, Sunday brunches, and ladies' luncheons. I got over it, though, much like a fever. I am currently more interested in simple, fast, no-fuss food. Even salads seem like a lot of work. My sister loves to make salads—chopping, cleaning, slicing, peeling. She is right at home in May, National Salad Month. When we were young, green salads in our small town meant a wedge of iceberg lettuce with a dollop of dressing on top. A salad supper at church would feature a half-dozen macaroni salads and even more Jell-O salads. The list is endless of ingredients that can go into molded Jell-O salads.

And what is it about us that likes lists so much? Americans love list-making.

I read a readers' survey in *Ladies' Home Journal* about the list of people we would most like to have for a dinner party, ten people in this order: President George W. Bush, Robin Williams, Oprah Winfrey, Laura Bush, Caroline Kennedy Schlossberg, Bill Cosby, Pope John Paul II, Jennifer Aniston, Katie Couric, and J. K. Rowling. Have those readers lost their minds? Surely they didn't mean they would like to have those ten people all at once. To me that sounds like the dinner party from hell. Jennifer Aniston and the pope? Oprah and Robin Williams? There is not enough herbal tea in the western hemisphere to get me through a dinner like that.

But I still like lists. When I was booking ballet tours, I learned that there are three phases to a contract—three things the sponsors say to you when trying to make the deal:

1. "No problem."
2. "Yes, but . . ."
3. "Oh, by the way . . ."

It goes this way. Perhaps I was saying that we absolutely positively could not perform without twelve local stagehands. Signing the contract depends on the sponsor providing twelve local stagehands. It is not negotiable. "No problem," the person tells me, full of confidence. So we sign the contract.

Just before we set out on the road, I call to make sure that all is well and that everything in the contract is under compliance, including the twelve local stagehands, which they agreed to provide. "Yes, we agreed to do that, but . . ." and then there's some excuse, some problem that is standing in the way. But I am firm. Got to have twelve local stagehands.

It is essential. The show cannot go on without it. I am so adamant, the sponsor agrees.

Until we arrive and then the other shoe is dropped, which is the third stage of the contract: "Oh, by the way—we could get only three stagehands. And they're boys from the junior high band."

But I still have hope for lists. In my dreams I will meet a man who is not only Mr. Right but even Mr. Perfect, and after fulfilling all the basic criteria, he will tell me that he has four things he wants to tell me:

1. He loves to cook.
2. His hobby is handyman repairs around the house.
3. He is a trained masseur.
4. He likes to dance.

Four things. Is that too much to ask?

June

Summer laid her simple Hat
On its boundless Shelf—

—Emily Dickinson, from poem 1363

The Flower of June Is the Rose

My Little Garden of Toughies

One summer I read an extraordinarily good Hollywood memoir—
The Memory of All That by Betsy Blair, who was Gene Kelly's first wife.
She was a red-haired, eighteen-year-old dancer from New Jersey audi-
tioning for a Billy Rose cabaret show in New York where the choreog-
rapher happened to be twenty-eight-year-old Gene Kelly. They married.
She was a child-bride in Hollywood for sixteen years, acted in the
movie *The Snakepit* with Olivia De Havilland and was the starring
female role in *Marty* with Ernest Borgnine, and then was blacklisted
because of her leftist political views. Her Hollywood career was over
and so was that life.

She fell in love with a French actor, left the United States, and began
a new life in Paris, acting in European films and mingling with French
intelligentsia. After some years of success, she left *that* life to marry film
director Karel Reisz and make a new life in London with more stage
work and more European intellects.

She moved on. She had vigor and courage.

Betsy Blair has reinvented herself at least four times. She tells all of
this—her life, her hard knocks, her affairs, her career—without guilt or
rancor. She says: This is what happened, this is what I thought at the
time, this is what happened next, this is what I think now—and that's
the way life is.

About the same time, I discovered that in South Africa a rose was
named for Helen Suzman on the occasion of her eighty-fifth birthday.
Helen Suzman is a tiny Jewish political activist. For thirty-six years,
she was the lone voice in South Africa's parliament speaking up
against apartheid. I met her at a cocktail party in her very smart home

in Johannesburg, and I asked her, "How did you find the courage?" She said, "I didn't need courage—I needed stamina."

This inspired me to start a new rose garden filled with roses named for tough, courageous, interesting women. Cleopatra, Ingrid Bergman, Lady Godiva—all have roses named for them. I am ordering a "Helen Suzman," which is small, creamy pink, hardy, and full of thorns. Quite appropriate, since she was a thorn in the side of the South African government.

Roses must like to be named. In the sixth century B.C., the Greek poet Sappho proclaimed the rose to be the Queen of Flowers. Naming roses for people has a long tradition. The "Madame Hardy" rose, named for the wife of Empress Josephine's head gardener, was hybridized in 1832 in France. It is a fine damask rose.

In my garden's entertainment section, I will have "Barbra Streisand," a pure mauve rose with a fragrance described as ravishing; "Marilyn Monroe," creamy apricot; "Elizabeth Taylor," bright deep pink with deeper edges; and "Dolly Parton," orange-red and described as "large and well-formed." I will order a "Judy Garland," a three-foot yellow floribunda rosebush produced by British rose grower R. Harkness and Company. Yellow roses were Miss Garland's favorite.

According to Pat Losiewicz, a devoted Garland fan grieving the singer's sudden death, getting this rose named in Miss Garland's memory was an ordeal. It took eight years (1970–1978) to accomplish. Jackson and Perkins, the world's largest rose grower, politely declined three times, saying that the company was busy naming a rose in memory of Jeanette MacDonald, so Miss Losiewicz turned to the English rose company.

I will not order "Jeanette MacDonald," because I was never a fan of her singing, but I will plant "Maria Callas," "Lilli Marlene," "Charlotte Rampling," and "Queen Nefertiti." Now there is a quartet that can hold its own.

I will not mix modern politics with gardening. Just think what that would do to the soil. Consequently, I will not have a "Barbara Bush" or a "Rosalyn Carter."

Unlike endorsing tennis shoes and designer clothes, famous people do not get paid to have a rose named for them. It is an honor. The American Rose Society and the international registering authority require permission from the famous person or his or her estate. Once named, the rose name is registered as a trademark and the rose is patented.

The rest of us can pay for the privilege. Buy our way in to the garden. Tip the gardener. The cost with Jackson and Perkins is $75,000.

I wish there were a rose named for Betsy Blair. One of her friends asked her about all the changes she has made in her life. "How did you find the courage?" the friend asked her. And Miss Blair said, "Every change I made, I did it for love."

I do not have a rose named for me, but when I was a restaurant critic, an Oklahoma City restaurant named a hamburger in my honor. It came with all the trimmings—lettuce, tomato, mustard, and pickles. I like that. I want all the trimmings in life.

After reading Miss Blair's memoir, I am planning on reinventing myself. I am moving on. From a hamburger I may go as high as a rose. Currently, I am in a dreamy Carole Lombard period. I float around my house wearing gold silk pajamas and a lilac kimono. I listen to Edith Piaf sing about love and life. I drink vodka gimlets stirred with a black-lacquered chopstick.

I do not have a definite plan, but I have a design for my little garden of toughies. I am ready for change. Whatever it is, I am going to do it with courage and love. I hope I also do it with vigor so that I, like my roses, can stick around for a while.

Father's Day Is the Third Sunday in June

Father's Day

Father's Day may seem to have been around forever, like Christmas or the Fourth of July, but it is a relatively new holiday. The idea was first celebrated in 1910 in Spokane, Washington. In 1924, Calvin Coolidge supported the idea of a national Father's Day, but not until 1966 did Lyndon Johnson declare by presidential proclamation that the third Sunday in June be observed as Father's Day. It has come to mean a day to honor fathers, stepfathers, uncles, grandfathers, teachers—all men who act as father figures.

My father's name was Joe. A strong name, a common man-on-the-street, synonym-for-coffee name. Joe America, Everyday Joe, G.I. Joe, Cuppa Joe. It is one of my favorite names.

That Father's Day comes in June is particularly appropriate for me. Of all the seasons, I associate my father most closely with summer. My father was a man of high energy, good spirits, and a sense of fun, all embodied in summer activity. Summer was a time for family swimming parties at a river with all my cousins or fishing at the lake.

I must have been a great trial to him on our outings. Once I managed to step into the coffee they were cooking in a big can; my whole foot was in the can. Another time I picked a bouquet of poison ivy. I do not recommend this. I was so nearsighted that even with my little pink-framed glasses, I could never see the hawk or squirrel he was pointing out. "Where, where?" I would ask. "Right there," he would answer. "Christ Almighty." I never saw anything but big blue skies and blurry green trees.

Closer to home, barbecuing in the backyard was a family ritual. The rest of us sliced tomatoes, made baked beans, cut the watermelon, and cranked homemade ice cream, but barbecuing the meat was my father's job, more of a right than a skill. Whatever the meat, it ended up the same—barbecued beyond recognition and slathered with sauce.

My father was a great reader, reading far into the night. One hot summer night as I lay reading in my bedroom with the windows open, I heard a male voice at the window whisper, "I'm coming in." The sound was so sinister, I stopped breathing. My heart popped and then I screamed, "Daddy!" Somehow, two rooms away, he knew what was happening. In one motion, he leapt from his chair in the living room where he sat reading, grabbed a loaded shotgun, stubbed his toe on the way out the front door, and blew the top out of the pecan tree. As he told the story later, when the gun went off, the divorcée's house across the street was alive with men jumping out windows. My window-peeper was caught that same night.

My father was a patient whittler, carving peach pits into monkeys and rectangles of pine into complex interlocking puzzles. Once he whittled me a slingshot, which I broke immediately by pulling it against a fence post. He made me wooden stilts, and one winter, a sled.

Mostly I remember him as a man of action. He was a lineman for the electric company for thirty-five years. I never remember him calling in sick or complaining about his job. Surely he did, but I do not remember it. I think about this sometimes with shame when I hear myself whining about work or lying in bed with a headache and a cold pack.

What I remember is his going to work with his lunch in a metal pail, year in and year out, in all kinds of weather, providing for his family. In the summer, he came home from work, mowed the lawn, and planted a garden, growing everything from summer staples such as new potatoes and green beans to peanuts for fun.

On winter weekends he went hunting and was a crack shot with quail, duck, squirrels, and rabbits. He trained his bird dogs to point and fetch. But in the summer, after work, he went fishing. He was a great bass and crappie fisherman.

He was patient with fishing poles and bean poles and training morning glories to climb a trellis, but one thing ignited his quick Irish temper, and that was his mortal enemy the lawn mower. Every year, on a Saturday spring morning, he went to the garage, whistling and merry, to tune the lawn mower. He rolled it out, cleaned it, oiled it, filled it with fuel, then tried to start it. Nothing. Again and again he yanked the starter. A seething silence fell over the backyard and the rest of us disappeared. The next thing we heard was an explosion of temper and cursing and crashing. Once we looked out the kitchen window to see him swinging an ax at the lawn mower. "Oh look," my little sister said, "Daddy is tuning the lawn mower. He's tuning it to smithereens." The next step was a trip to the hardware store to buy a new lawn mower, this one positively guaranteed. Why is it that he could keep an outboard fishing motor humming for years but couldn't get a lawn mower to work two summers in a row?

He called me Princess, but he taught me to play poker. When I was about twelve, he once sent me away from the table because I did not open with a pair of jacks. He was critical of my beaux and was fond of saying, "I've seen more intelligent heads on a nickel beer."

He had no sons, so in the summer, he coached a teenage baseball team and bought armloads of fireworks for the Fourth of July to amuse his two daughters.

My father bought me my first piece of jewelry, a miniature pair of silver paratrooper wings. It was during World War II; I had just been born, and my father, a member of the 508th Parachute Infantry, came home on leave to meet me.

He whooped and hollered when he was square dancing, he loved to tease, and he was fearless. It was family legend how he had come upon a car accident with people trapped inside as the car started to burn. A crowd gathered to watch, but only my father kicked out the windows and pulled the people out to safety before the car exploded. I saw that same rush to action one summer when I almost drowned at Noel, Missouri. People stood in shallow water and watched me go under. My sister yelled for my father with a voice like a siren, and from out of nowhere my father rushed into the water like the cavalry, pulled me to safety, and then turned his full fury on the meek onlookers. His temper with the lawn mower paled in comparison. He was so vehement with the "cowardly sons of bitches" that they slunk out of the water, got into their cars, and drove away from the vacation spot.

He was not perfect and was sometimes too harsh and too quick to punish his young daughters, but that same fearless rush to action was what made him a superb volunteer fireman for our small town. Maybe it is having inherited his temper that makes me tend to keep score in times of emotional crisis. At his funeral, I was enraged to not see other volunteer firemen at the service. He had served that fire department for thirty years, and they couldn't come pay their respects? Then, as the funeral procession pulled away from the church and headed toward the cemetery, there on the side of the highway I saw the fire truck, washed and shined with the lights flashing, and, standing beside it at attention, the town's volunteer firemen. They saluted as the hearse drove by. I cannot remember this sweet scene—the elderly firemen straining to stand tall—without weeping.

Father's Day is the third Sunday of June, the month that also fittingly includes D-day (the great Allied invasion) and Little League Baseball Day. And the fourth Sunday of June is National Forgiveness Day, a day to forgive and forget and set ourselves free of old grievances, including childhood grievances toward fathers.

June Is the Month of Weddings

Spring Mergers

I love our pagan roots. However we traipse around intellectualizing and modernizing, we are still primitives in fancy dress. A hairsbreadth from squatting on our haunches around a campfire gnawing on the shank of a musk ox.

Consider June weddings, for example. In the United States, some 2.5 million weddings are performed annually, and a good number of them in June. We may think it is because of nice weather and abundant flowers or perhaps because this was once a slack time between planting and harvesting when people had time to get married. In truth, an underlying reason for this romantic tradition is an ancient superstition. May weddings were considered bad luck. May was the month when we commemorated the dead, not a jolly time to get married. May was the month of Roman sexual festivals and Celtic fertility ceremonies. May was the month when gods and goddesses coupled, and nobody wanted to compete with the deities.

In Europe, the only full moon of June was known as the Honey Moon, a time to gather honey from the hives, and thus the wedding holiday became known as the honeymoon. Who knows if that is true. Elsewhere, June's full moon is called the Strawberry Moon, the Rose Moon, and the Flower Moon. Among the Cherokees, it is the Green Corn Moon. Nobody writes romantic songs about the Green Corn Moon. What rhymes with corn? Horn, mourn, scorn, torn, thorn, outworn. Not in the same category as June, moon, and swoon.

Stir it all together, smooth it over with a few centuries of culture, and the custom of June weddings prevails.

Last June I was hunched over my computer, panting and perspiring and struggling to master something with labels while people kept calling to tell me they were getting married. These were not mere acquaintances, mind you, these were people I care about. Some of them I am related to. I realize that weddings are life-changing news, but still—I had this computer problem with labels and addresses.

A young man and his fiancée were both on the phone burbling in stereo about the proposal and the ring and the dress and the reception and the caterer and the guest list. Without a breath they segued into plans for a house and a baby and his stuff and her stuff.

I thought, "How many times have I heard this? From how many people?" Nothing much about My Beloved or Mr. Right, but long strands of talk about ceremony and ritual and stuff. It made me feel so old and tired, I could hardly gin up the right responses. I felt like an old biddy sitting on the porch in a rocking chair watching the parade of life going by and weakly waving a little flag.

At present, my life is far removed from romantic flurry. I have different things on my mind. I realized just how different when I spent a Friday night rhapsodizing over a new mop. How thrilling, I thought, to have a newly designed mop that works. How exciting to discover a new concept in mopping. How pathetic! How low is my threshold of entertainment?

It is not that I do not know it is spring. How could I not know it, with all that riotous bird activity outside my office window, flapping and chirping and pairing off and building nests and opening joint accounts everywhere? There is even a little nest in my rosebush.

And all the spring flowers bursting into blowsy bloom. I know that is not for my delight. It is flagrant, floral sexuality. The blooms are Mother Nature's way of saying, "Come close and see me sometime."

I know all of that, and I appreciate it. It is what makes the world go around. But the thing with my computer was really difficult. Where was my data? What does "merge field" mean?

About that time, the phone rang and someone was calling on a cell phone from the Grand Canyon to tell me that they were getting married. They were monumentally happy and exuberant, shouting the details at me. Valentine's Day. In Memphis. At the Chapel of Love. Staying across the street at Heartbreak Hotel. Do I need to explain that they are Elvis fans?

I said, "That's lovely, really lovely, but let me ask you something, do you know how to do labels?"

I do not know if they do or not, because the phone reception was awful. Unless they hung up.

Here is what I think. Getting married is hard. Staying married is harder. But none of it is as hard as mail merge.

I mean, what is a catalog in my computer and why don't I have an address book and what is Microsoft exchange? All I want is to print labels from a page of addresses. Even if it is spring, that is what I want.

A mockingbird in my neighborhood has a voice like Ethel Merman and a repertoire of about thirty tunes. Every morning at 4:30, he parks himself outside my bedroom window and belts them out. I thought he was looking for a mate, a little hen to call his own, and I wished to heaven that he would find one so I could get some sleep. Then I thought, maybe he's singing in joy because he has found a mate and they have the caterer lined up.

No, nobody would sing that robustly for that long about a wedding. I suspect the truth is that the mockingbird has mastered mail merge. He has printed labels (without phone numbers, mind you), and he is moving smartly to the address book. Now that is something to sing about.

June Is Adopt-a-Cat Month

Cats and Wax

When I was just out of college and young and foolish, there was a dreadful episode and my heart was broken.

I do not want to suggest that youth is the only time our hearts get broken. We all get older and sometimes wiser, but I think our hearts should stay young and foolish and ready to take risks. At the time of this story I am telling now, I happened to be young, and my heart was broken, and my spirits were flattened. I was sitting listlessly in my brown, furnished postcollege apartment staring straight ahead when a friend showed up at my door with two bottles and some advice.

One was a bottle of wine. She sat down and shared it with me. The other bottle she left with me. It was a bottle of lemon wax. This was her advice: "Now get up and start cleaning house because you can't be depressed when the house smells like lemon wax." Of all the advice I've received through the years, this ranks among the top.

Currently I am going through a feng shui–zen phase, and I want surfaces to be clear and shiny. It keeps me calm and more productive. I am not always as high minded and tidy. This spartan phase comes on the heels of leaving the ironing board set up in the living room for two weeks.

In movies, people with a peck of trouble sit at bars and tell their woes to bartenders. Sometimes women confide in their hairdresser. Me, I go to my veterinarian or to my favorite pet store, lean on the counter, and pour out my heart. That is because most of my troubles these days are about my cat. I have a wonderful yellow-and-white cat named Louie who looks exactly like Russell Crowe with sad eyes that turn down at the corners. But this naughty cat has begun spraying things in the house. Cat people know about spraying. The rest of the world does not need to know this dark side of the feline world. Spraying is just one of the reminders that the word "domesticated" is a myth about cats.

So, Louie has been spraying windows, doors, fireplace, and worst of all, my computer. I confess that there are days when I feel the same way about the computer, but this is not acceptable behavior. Although I adore this yellow cat, this is a tedious problem. Not only do I spend a lot of time cleaning house, it is potentially costly. I remember how expensive it was when my cat Phoebe threw up in the phone-answering/fax machine.

I was repeating this lamentation in the pet-supply store the other day when another woman joined the conversation. "Oh, cat troubles," she said. "Do I know cat troubles. And I keep attracting more cats. Why can't I attract other things the way I attract cats—diamonds, for example? If I could attract men and money the way I attract cats, I'd be a happier woman."

Great, deep question. Why do we attract the things we attract? Why do we behave the way we do? Ah, sweet mysteries of life. And oh, the lure of vertical surfaces. Where is that old friend when I need her? The one with all the answers and the bottle of lemon wax.

June Is the Official Start of Summer

Suntan

A writing professor told me that men and women tell stories differently. Women tell them chronologically. A woman might start a story this way: "This morning I had to go down Seventy-first Street on an errand, and since I was in that area, I thought I would stop at that really good bakery and you'll never guess who I saw having coffee at a corner table." A woman unwinds a story as if it were a new ball of yarn.

But a man telling the same story would start with the punch line: "Guess who I saw having coffee together this morning? Jim and Sandra." A man rips open a story like a package.

With that gender storytelling mode in mind, here is how I got into my current dilemma. It all started when I bought a new pair of summer sandals. And a kicky chiffon skirt in a fuchsia color. Now what I need, I said to myself, are bare shiny legs and—not a suntan exactly, but a kissed-by-the-sun golden glow. That is the problem. I have no golden glow. I am so pale, I look like a flounder. And long gone are the days when I would lie baking in the sun, slowly turning my skin into the texture of an old alligator purse.

The solution, I reasoned as shrewdly as an international chess champion, is an artificial tan—suntan in a tube. I have tried this before, with sad results, but surely products have been improved since then. I understand that there are now suntan sprays. Plus, I have become more patient and methodical. This time will be different. That is always my mantra as I set off on some harebrained project: "This time will be different."

I stood at the cosmetics counter staring wistfully at the suntan cream while the clerk watched me the way my cat watches a fat bug creep by. "I've tried these before," I told the clerk, "and the problem is, the color comes out streaked." I wanted her to know I was no pushover. I was a cynical hard sell. Nobody was going to put anything over on me. I had bought cosmetics before, and lots of them.

"Oh, I know just the solution," she said brightly. "First you use this exfoliating scrub and then the skin is polished so smoothly, the color will be perfect."

"Sold," I said. "Give me both."

So I bought not one but two products in the dream of getting a golden glow. That is one of the secrets of advertising—we believe what we want to believe. And I wanted to believe it would work.

Industriously—that is how I polished and exfoliated. Carefully— that is how I applied the suntan cream, rubbing first one way and then crossways because I am not as slapdash as I once was. Hours passed with no change in color, but that did not bother me. I am more patient now. Contentedly—that's how I drifted off to sleep, knowing that I would wake up with a been-to-the-Greek-isles suntanned look.

Wrong. Again. I woke up as splotched and streaked as ever. My whole body looked as if I had been tie-died in strong coffee. I thought this would be a light tan, but it was as if I started slathering on dark stage makeup for a role in *South Pacific,* wandered off to answer the phone, and forgot what I was doing.

My body was speckled tan. Except for my feet, which were orange. I was the spitting image of Daisy Duck.

Well, there was another self-improvement project run aground. Although I guess "self-improvement" is not an accurate description, since it was driven solely by vanity. I remembered all the other home improvement and get-great-quick schemes that had gone off the rails. Home hair coloring is at the top of the list. Amateur plumbing repair is another memorable event. So is paint touch-up on my car. The leitmotif of my life is "How did I get into this mess?"

And why is it that these projects are never fixed as easily as they are broken? My old friend the exfoliating scrub did not help with this botched fake suntan. It just made the pale places paler. The solution was socks until the color wore off.

I am going to try another tack. I am going to change my perception. What is so great about a suntan? The look of delicate dusting powder is just as attractive. Perhaps I will carry a small, fringed parasol. I hope I have more luck with changing my mind than I had with changing my pallor.

The Summer Solstice Is June 21 or June 22

Wish You Weren't Here

Mercifully, we have lurched past the summer equinox, the day the sun appears to stand still in the sky at noon. The word comes from the Latin *sol,* "sun," and *sistit,* "stands." The summer solstice is the longest day and the shortest night of the year.

This means we are halfway through summer and, what is even more important, halfway through summer vacations.

I had a postcard from friends on vacation and all it said was, "I wish we had stayed home and thought about coming here."

Last winter I visited my sister and brother-in-law in Tucson, and it was great—being shown around town, touring Mission San Xavier del Bac, eating at the locals' favorite Mexican restaurants. I had so much fun that I insisted that they come to Tulsa to visit. I begged. I bribed them with tickets to the jazz festival. I pouted until they accepted.

That was February. I am over it now. But they came anyway, although every cell in my body cried out: Turn back!

Suddenly everything in my house looked grungy. Oh, the cleaning, the gardening, the great moving of furniture at midnight. And the shopping—those special organic soft drinks they like. A new slipcover for the garden room chair. At least I was not obsessive enough to have the chair reupholstered. I tried but there was not time to get it done. The fabric I bought is stored in the garage.

I was exhausted even before they got here, and the holiday fun was just beginning.

"Welcome, welcome," I cried oh so insincerely. "I have some of those organic soft drinks you like already chilled and waiting for you."

"Oh, we don't drink those anymore," my sister said.

Great. Three six-packs of organic lemonade that none of us drink.

"Do you have any bottled spring water?" she asked.

"No," I said, "but we can stop and get some." By then we were in the car starting a three-day marathon of sightseeing around town. On vacation, we want to pack in as much fun as we can.

What we did was shop for Indian art, shop for Indian jewelry, shop for University of Oklahoma memorabilia, eat out every meal, eat barbecue in the south side, eat barbecue in the north side, buy more bottled spring water, carry home bags of pastry, drive out of town to see the scenery, have an allergic reaction to said scenery, need special medication for the allergic reaction, take our photos with all the painted penguins in town, realize that the film was not loaded properly in the camera, retrace our steps, and retake our photos with all the painted penguins in town. And, of course, the big event—attend the jazz festival.

Leave the jazz festival early because the sound is loud and giving some of us a headache. Shop for more Indian art, and—saving the best for the last—visit Oral Roberts University, architecture my sister describes as a collection of bowling trophies. Take our photograph under the giant praying hands. Meet visitors who couldn't speak English and take their photograph under the giant praying hands.

After my guests went back to Arizona where they belong, I took to my bed for a long, recuperative nap. When I awoke, I remembered that my friends in Boston have been begging me to come visit them. Begging me.

So I called them and said I would be there Friday. They are expecting twins in a couple of months, and I want to get the visit in before the babies arrive.

"But," I told them, "I absolutely do not want to be a bother, so be brutally truthful. Are you sure this is a good time?"

After what seemed like a long delay—probably something mechanical—they said, "The time is perfect. Come ahead."

What fun. I can't wait to see Boston. Eat seafood. Shop. Maybe drive to the Cape . . .

July

A something in a summer's noon—
A depth—an Azure—a perfume—
Transcending ecstasy.

—Emily Dickinson, from poem 122

July 1 Is Mr. Zip Day

Titles of Address

Okay, get your pencil, because this is complicated.

I thought we would talk today about the proper forms of address.

Now, say you want to write to the queen of England. How do you address her? Your Majesty? Aha, that's where you are wrong. You do not write a letter directly to the queen. You address the envelope to her private secretary. Inside, you can call her Your Majesty.

But that was a trick question.

This all started when I was writing a letter to a bishop and wondered if I should address him as Bishop So-and-So or as Your Grace. I am glad I looked it up because Your Grace would have been entirely wrong. It is just Bishop. Bishop Smith, if he is Protestant or Episcopalian. Or, if Roman Catholic, it could be Your Excellency.

The envelope is what is hard. For an Episcopalian, address the envelope to The Right Reverend, and for a Roman Catholic, address it to The Most Reverend. Sometimes a salutation on the letter could be The Right Reverend Sir. You will notice that we hardly ever have to worry about addressing female bishops of any faith.

So I began meandering among the rules for correct forms of address. I love the way humans take something—anything—and detail it to a fare-thee-well. We can make elaborate ceremonies and rituals out of almost anything.

Such as titles.

Here are some examples. Write these down, because they are tricky.

For Popes: Your Holiness or Most Holy Father.

For Cardinals: Your Eminence.

Rabbis are easy. It is just Dear Rabbi Smith.

But if you are addressing an Orthodox Patriarch, it is either Your Holiness for the Russian Orthodox or Your All Holiness for the Greeks.

Let us move on, out of religion.

If you have need to communicate properly with a British titled personage, well, you have your work cut out for you.

Lady Margaret Russell, a Maid of Honor and an earl's daughter, can be called Lady Margaret or Mistress Russell but never Lady Russell and never ever Lady Margaret Mistress Russell. Only an oaf would make that blunder. Good Lord.

Actually, the eldest son of an earl is called Lord So-and-So. The title of Lord is only for a baron or better. A duchess, of course, is called Your Grace, and the wife of a baronet is called Lady So-and-So. But so is a countess, who is the wife of an earl.

I recommend corresponding only with Americans because it is considerably easier. Here, everybody is Mr. or Mrs. or Madame—Mr. President, Madame Justice. Or by job title—Judge Jones, Governor Jones, or Mayor Jones.

And yet, one of the biggest dustups I remember was about titles in the United States in the 1970s, and it was the new title of Ms. It was an effort at nonsexist language. Since all males, married or unmarried, were called Mr., it seemed only fair that women did not have to be known by our marital status. This wasn't exactly a new idea. Back in 1948, Elizabeth Cady Stanton urged women to use neither Miss nor Mrs. but only their first and last names.

But oh, my. Such a fuss. When *Ms.* magazine was introduced, the name alone made it seem daring. Many people felt that feminists were declaring war on marriage. I quit going to one doctor because the office insisted on either a Miss or a Mrs. title and when I refused to be called either, the office manager told me, "Well, I'm proud that I'm married."

What is it about marriage, then and now, that ignites such battles? If you want to throw a conversational stink bomb into a gathering, just introduce the subject of same-sex marriage.

An academic paper that I read recently said that Ms. is still misunderstood. Not just a neutral term like Mr., it seems to identify a woman as a single female or a career-oriented woman. I thought that was long settled, but that just shows you how wrong a Ms. can be.

And that is our little lesson today in forms of address.

Yours sincerely

P.S. Mr. Zip Day commemorates the introduction of the zip code July 1, 1963, when a first-class stamp was five cents.

Fourth of July

What Did You Do?

Here's what my friends did over the Fourth of July:

Drove to Memphis to visit family

Had a neighborhood party in the small park, with hotdogs, hamburgers, and games for the kids

Invited the whole family over for barbecue

Took a picnic to watch the fireworks display

Baked a red-white-and-blue pie with fresh berries

Attended an outdoor concert

Bicycled and hiked

Boated on the lake

Here is what I did:

Sank into plumy, summer afternoon naps

Strung Chinese lanterns in a tree

Sat outside under a red Japanese umbrella and ate cherries, letting the pits fall into the grass

Watched three starlings march in stride across the lawn

Snapped green beans from the farmers market and cooked them with new potatoes

Smelled the fragrant lavender at twilight

Brought in the U.S. flag at nightfall

It was a heavenly holiday weekend.

July 10 Is Clerihew Day

Slugging It Out with Words

I think of myself as a word collector. I like them separately, strung together in sentences or quotations, and in great lengths, like yard goods, made into articles and books.

Collecting words is a lazy woman's hobby. It is as rewarding to me as collecting silver, but somebody else does the polishing. I'm a sucker for the well-turned phrase.

- From a poem by E. E. Cummings: "The snow doesn't give a soft white damn whom it touches."
- From a book review, author long forgotten: "This is the way a writer dies—impaled on his own imagination."
- From James Thurber: "Urge up a footstool, loosen your stays, and saucer your scotch."
- From a Lyle Lovett song: "Go where your heart says go."

Muscling my own words into shape for market is harder. Some days it's like sculpting granite with Popsicle sticks. The few words I can think of sit on the page as heavy as stone. I shove at the immovable block of copy, trying to chisel life into its sullen weight. If weeping would help, I'd do it. Sometimes I do it anyway.

Other days, the words fall as stardust from my fingertips to the keyboard. The sentences stand *en pointe* and do pirouettes on the page. Every line sprints as elegantly as a wire-to-wire Triple Crown winner. The next day I come back to the office to read this silken prose and the blood drains from my face. What happened to it overnight? It is so bad, I am queasy and have to lie down. Then I get up and fight back.

Those are the days when I wish I communicated through numbers. The language on the other side of the fence looks greener and easier. I

envy the clarity of the invoice from my Vietnamese typewriter repairman: "Cat pee in typewriter—$50.00." There may or may not be a verb
in that invoice, but there is no question about the cost. Or the problem.

Someone said that the man never lived who could dash off a
Gettysburg Address on the back of an envelope. The trick was to make
it look dashed off—not to let the work show, not to reveal the effort,
not to let anyone see you gnaw on desk legs, hit the equipment, or
cover your face and whimper. For writers, words are both the prey and
the weapon.

"Prayers" is a funny, clever, and well-written essay by novelist Mary
Gordon. Mirroring the high-stepping language of a time gone by, she
writes prayers "For Those Who Devote Themselves to Personal
Adornment," "For Those Who Have Given Up Everything for Sexual
Love," and—one of my favorites—"For Those Who Misuse or Do Not
Use or Cannot Use Their Gifts." The last prayer petitions new direction
"for conservatory-trained composers of incidental music, for athletes
who watch television, for poets who write commercials, for cat-lovers
afraid of mess."

I tried to sit outside this summer on Sunday afternoons and read or
write in a journal. The neighbors' arduous lawn work shattered all con-
centration. One obsessive neighbor mowed, blowed, and edged for six
hours. How straight does the grass line have to be along the sidewalk?
A religious fanatic on his craziest day could not have been more zeal-
ous than this man was about saving his lawn from untidiness.

I closed my book and tried to compose spiteful clerihews about the
gardener. A clerihew is a four-lined verse about a person. Clerihews are
supposed to be funny. Mine were not only bad but also as mean spirited as if I had written them with a nail.

> A neighbor I'll leave anonymous
> Heaps loud misery upon us
> I hope and I pray
> That he'll move far away.

> The man who lives next door
> Has such a loud power blower
> I wish he were so inclined
> To stuff it up his behind.

This was getting me nothing but bad karma, so I scrambled to higher ground and, inspired by Mary Gordon, wrote my own prayer of supplication.

A Prayer for Those with a Gift for Noise

O God, for all those with mowers, blowers, edgers, grinders, Shop-Vacs, and all other yard equipment that makes a mighty noise, grant them the gift of silence, perhaps the epiphany of reading and sitting quietly. Give them, I beseech thee, no knowledge of a portable radio. If it pleases thee, gift them with a temporary affliction that keeps them indoors. And for those blessed with a barking dog, grant them compassion on us, thy neighbors, and also upon the dog. Grant the dog access to their house, likewise a big pig's ear to chew so that we, the irritated neighbors, shall be relieved of ill temper, quit of our snarling and glaring and, yea, even cursing. And over all—thy people and dogs and yard machines—let peace be restoreth, tranquility reigneth, and silence prevail. And start, I humbly beseech thee, in my neighborhood. Amen.

July 11 Is National
Cheer Up the Lonely Day

Look, Jane, Look and See

I am not a melancholy person, but I have come to value funerals even though they make me weepy. Maybe because they make me weepy.

It is all too easy to get pulled into the grind of everyday life with its vexations: the workload that mounds higher and higher above my head, the unexpected expense that hits like a body blow, the recurring problem with the printer, the rascally cat who hides and won't come in. And the dreary daily chores that drone on like a gong solo: the insufferable weather, the aches and pains of the body, the ungrateful person who doesn't say "thank you." I am a walking Gilbert and Sullivan song: I've got a little list. I've got them on my list.

And then—a funeral jars me to a halt, moves me to another awareness.

I gather with other mourners for this ancient ritual. I survey the congregation, taking roll in my personal book of judgment. I am small and mean spirited as I note who is absent and who is missing that ought to be here. Sometimes I count the number of floral tributes. I peek ashamedly to see how grief has wracked the family.

Gradually my heart opens and I notice details of sweet pain. At one funeral, the congregation was almost entirely old women. At another, only one person walked behind the casket—Patti, an only child burying her mother. At a funeral in late summer, I heard a eulogy of plain tenderness. It was a love story.

Mary Frances and Donald Hayden were both teachers who shared a devotion of faith, literature, and poetry, especially Elizabeth Barrett and Robert Browning. They met in high school; she was his English teacher. They had been married sixty-two years, and before that, they had courted for eight years. Seventy years together, sundered by her death.

Dr. Hayden was one of my university professors. He is a Wordsworth scholar, and he taught Shakespeare for thirty years. It was natural that he would help fashion a funeral service filled with poetry. As the funeral rolled on, I felt myself suspended between two seasons: summer and fall. Between the temporal and the spiritual. Between reality TV and nineteenth-century poetry.

A *Newsweek* article about the cost of this Information Age says that we have data and speed as never before. We are wired to information with cell phones and pagers and laptops and e-mails. The one thing we do not have is time. The article said, "If your brain is always multi-tasking and responding to technoprompts, there is no time or energy for undirected mental play." We overcommunicate, and that means we do not have time to read or to think. Or to create. Because creativity usually happens while we are doing something else, when the brain has the time to experiment its way to something new.

Who in this age has the time or patience to read poetry? But at the funeral we did. We sang hymns. We said prayers. And we listened to the minister read Browning.

I got weepy, being grateful for my circles of community. For the car rental office that called to say they had found my address book. For the tailor shop where the seamstress said, "Why, honey, you're not as big as a minute." For the bookstore clerk who teases me about the risks of carpal tunnel syndrome and shopping. "Repetitive motion, you know," he says, "swiping credit cards through the charge machine so often."

The mourners filed out past the church's day school, where children romped like puppies in the playground. How appropriate. The cycle of life—tears and laughter. I left the church vowing, yet again, to slow down and savor each day. To spoon it up.

So I took a plate of cookies to the new fire department in the neighborhood. And I remembered the funeral reading from Elizabeth Barrett Browning:

> Earth's crammed with heaven,
> And every common bush afire with God;
> But only he who sees, takes off his shoes;
> The rest sit round it and pluck blackberries.
>
> —*Aurora Leigh*, Book VII

Some time later, Dr. Hayden wrote me about life without Mary Frances. He shared with me a poem she had written to his mother:

Reminiscence

My husband's mother and I—
The fun we had
Exchanging arched-eyebrow glances
Behind the back of the man
We both adored!

Dr. Hayden's grief was still so raw that many things brought him to tears. Finally, he sent a poem that was much on his mind. The poem, by Sara Teasdale, is powerful standing alone, but read in the context of his loss, it is shattering.

The Lamp

If I can bear your love like a lamp before me,
When I go down the long, steep road of darkness,
   I shall not fear the everlasting shadows,
    Nor cry in terror.
If I can find out God, then I shall find Him.
If none can find Him, then I shall sleep soundly,
   Knowing how well on earth your love sufficed me,
    A lamp in darkness.

Cherokee Constitution Day, July 26 (1827), Is Also National Aunt and Uncle Day

Connie in Indian Land

It is not easy being anything—any race, ethnicity, sex, age, hair color —but it is uniquely difficult being a mixed-blood at American Indian functions.

I am careful to say that I am an *enrolled* member of the Cherokee Nation, which gives me some authenticity, and I am discreet in my wearing of turquoise, but even that does not protect me from being categorized as a wannabe. One year I was a speaker at a national meeting of Episcopal women. My talk was about the plight of urban Indians, a topic I had researched and written about. During the question and answer session, a woman from Alaska named Sally Twoblankets stepped to the microphone, and this was her question: "Why didn't they get a real Indian to speak?" The audience of some three thousand gasped at this public face slapping.

I have no illusions about my stature as a mixed-blood. At Indian functions, I am at the end of the table, below the salt. So I braced myself to go to the funeral of my uncle, Charles Greenfeather, a full-blood Shawnee. Many of those present were related to me by marriage, so they were friendly and welcoming. Still, I am an outsider when it comes to tribal ceremonies. At powwows I tend to commit gaucheries such as gawking at the dancers' regalia or talking through the honor songs.

I was not the only mixed-blood at the funeral, but most of the others were mixed Indian blood, which is a whole different enchilada than being mostly white. My cousin Carole Greenfeather's husband is Kiowa, Caddo, and Delaware; her handsome son-in-law is Seneca-Cayuga and

Creek. Her adopted brother, Randy, the spitting image of a young Cassius Clay, is Seneca from New York. The youngest person there was her grandson, a week-old boy whose Indian heritage is Wichita-Caddo, Delaware, Creek, Kiowa, Shawnee, and Cherokee. The bloodlines and the blood quantums are dizzyingly complicated to me, but the Indians know the detailed genealogies and remember them accurately, including who cannot legally claim association with a father's tribe because the parents were not married.

The service was rich with tribal ceremony. The funeral was a graveside ceremony in the family cemetery in Kansas, and it was full of tribal ceremony. At first, the casket was draped with the U.S. flag because my uncle was a great warrior and had fought in World War II campaigns in North Africa, Italy, France, and Germany. After a three-gun salute and the playing of taps, the flag was removed and the casket was opened and draped with an Indian blanket.

The Choctaw minister had us sing "Amazing Grace" in both English and Choctaw. My uncle had been dressed in his fanciest ribbon shirt and his gourd-dancing regalia—red-and-blue blanket, eagle-feather fan, and gourd. The corners of his eyes had been marked with a red stripe—lipstick, I found out later—to indicate that he was Shawnee. The family had tucked into the casket a little brown paper shopping basket with handles, full of snacks for his journey—Vienna sausage, cheese and crackers, beef jerky, cookies, and a soda. Not a diet soda, because now my uncle, who was diabetic, did not have to watch his sugar intake. He was free to eat whatever he wanted.

Then tribesmen came forward to conduct a Shawnee service. With knives they notched the casket so that my uncle's spirit could come and go. His burial had been scheduled for the fourth day after his death, and on this day, his journey began.

Indians are great believers in tobacco for ceremonial use, so we were invited to march by and sprinkle tobacco in the coffin. The people fell into a strict, segregated order: first male relatives, then male friends, followed by female relatives and, lastly, female friends. It had been some time since I had seen such a division of the sexes.

"Enjoy your exalted position," I said to Cordell Whitetree, a male relative, as he walked ahead of me, "because it won't last when we leave here."

"I know it." He laughed. "So I'm making the most of it."

To conclude the Shawnee ceremonial, the tribesman instructed us, "Stand and face the west. Then walk away. Because in our belief, we have now done all we can for him."

We reconvened to an Indian church where more ceremonies were to follow. Cedar was to be burned, and one by one, we could step into the smoke and be fanned by eagle feathers to take away all bad feelings and to sleep better. Bathing in cedar smoke would heal our grief.

This portion of the ceremony was delayed somewhat because the tribesmen could not get the charcoal briquettes to flame. Once again, we were automatically divided by sex. Women stood on one side of the little would-be fire, men on the other. While the Shawnees tried to get the fire going, the mourners passed the time taking photographs of one another. "No, turn the camera around; you're taking your own picture." "Wait—bunch in closer together—I don't have a wide-angle lens." These bungled photographic efforts evoked hearty laughter.

This problem with fire reminded me of attending the opening of the Trail of Tears drama in Tahlequah, the capital of the Cherokee Nation. This drama is held in an outdoors theater under a rising moon. I was accompanying Rennard Strickland, an Osage-Cherokee. He is such an eminent person among the tribes that he stopped to visit with everyone after the event, so we were the last to reach the parking lot. Or to try to reach it. We could not find our car in the woods. We could not even find the parking lot. We wandered through the thicket of trees as the night got darker and darker. At one point, Rennard said, "Face it. The tracking gene has been bred out of us."

Despite fifty years of marriage, my favorite aunt, the widow, remains decidedly non-Indian. Once the cedar was smoking, I asked her, "Auntie, do you want to do the smoke?"

"Oh Lord no," she said. "I don't understand this stuff."

I thought I had pushed my luck by participating in the tobacco ritual, so my aunt and I hung back, being very quiet and very white. When the cedar ceremony was concluded, we all retired into the church for a meal. Before we ate, however, more long prayers were offered, followed by a family give-away, in which individuals were called forward to receive hand-embroidered shawls or Pendleton blankets in gratitude for their service to my uncle and their help with the funeral.

The meal was typical Indian fare—platters of fried chicken, corn dishes, a giant pot of pinto beans and ham, and a table full of pies and cakes. Except for one tossed salad, I saw no fresh fruits or vegetables. The only fruit was grape dumplings to go with fry bread, a favorite Indian delicacy.

My friend Pam Iron (a Cherokee) was asked at one powwow if she had seen a certain person. "Last time I saw him," she said, "he was over there"—and she gestured across the way. "Eating a piece of fry bread as big as his face." When Pam went on a healthy regimen of exercise (which included jogging) and diet, she lost weight. Always her Indian colleagues greeted her with great concern. "You've lost weight," they would say sadly. "Have you been sick?" Despite their tendency to diabetes, Indians are often overweight, and it is unusual for Indians to lose weight by choice.

Carole's husband, Creighton Moore, is a large, regal man who weighs at least three hundred pounds. He is often selected to be arena director at powwows, a position of honor that acknowledges his authority and mastery of ceremony. At the postfuneral dinner, he passed by our table carrying in one hand a plate mounded with fry bread and two more pieces in his other hand. Carole watched him and then said to me, "Connie, if you want any fry bread, you'd better get it before it's all gone."

What a gesture of kinship, I thought. A peace offering from my cousin who scorned my Cherokee blood. And it has taken only fifty years. No time at all in Indian time.

Fry Bread Recipe

> 2 cups flour
> 3 teaspoons baking powder
> 1 teaspoon salt
> 2 cups milk or water
> A couple tablespoons of sugar (optional)

Mix flour, salt, and baking powder together. Add milk or water to make a soft dough. Turn onto floured board and pat to ½ inch thick. Cut into squares with a slit in the middle. Or dough can be pinched into a little ball and patted into size of a small saucer with a hole punched in the middle.

Fry in deep, hot fat—about 400 degrees (if too hot, bread will not cook in the middle). Brown on both sides. Drain on paper towel. Serve with honey, syrup, fruit, or grape dumplings.

Grape Dumplings

1 cup water
2 tablespoons melted shortening
1 teaspoon baking powder
2 cups flour
½ gallon unsweetened grape juice*
2 cups sugar

Mix water, shortening, and baking powder. Add flour to make a stiff dough. Roll out very thin on floured board. Cut into pieces 2" × ½". Add sugar to grape juice and bring to boil. Drop in dough pieces and cook 5 minutes uncovered at boiling heat, then simmer covered for 10 minutes.

*Variations: 1 quart grape juice, 1 quart canned grapes, and ¼ cup sugar. Or ½ quart fresh grapes with water to cover and sugar to taste. Or 1 can frozen grape juice, 2 cans water, and ⅓ to ⅔ cup sugar. Some cooks add a tablespoon of sugar to the dry mixture, use 4 teaspoons baking powder, add ¾ cup milk and cut in ⅓ cup margarine instead of using melted shortening.

August

As imperceptibly as Grief
The Summer lapsed away—

    —Emily Dickinson, from poem 1540

August 1 Is Friendship Day

Friends and Grandmothers

My friend Maridel sent me a greeting card with a color photograph of a championship chicken. "If you were a hen," she wrote, "this is the hen you would be. A glamour hen."

Maridel and I go to the opera together, and she thinks I overaccessorize. Still, it is surprising to have someone send you a picture of poultry. I should be getting used to it. I have a photograph of me with an eight-hundred-pound pig named Pork Chop. Her owner praised me mightily by saying, "I've never seen anyone bond with a pig like you do."

Even so, I have never thought of myself as a chicken. I read all about this little bird. It is called a Bearded Buff Laced Polish Large Fowl Hen—and she is a beauty with her crested, fancy topknot of feathers. This hen, I read, is a favorite at poultry exhibitions. All things considered, my friend could have a worse image of me.

I was at a meeting with a group of women forming a new social service foundation. "Before we begin," someone said, "do we need to agree on procedure for this discussion? Do we need to follow Robert's *Rules of Order?*"

"We don't need any rules," another woman said. "Let's just behave as if our grandmother was in the room."

Brilliant philosophy, I thought. Wouldn't the world run better if we all did that?

I thought about the advice my grandmother gave me. Mostly it was two things: "Don't talk bad about people" and "Sit up like a lady and keep your skirt down." These pearls are nothing I want to cross-stitch and hang on the wall, but maybe other grandmothers were more lyrical.

So I took a survey, asking people what wisdom they learned from their grandmothers. Some people had no useful recollection of wisdom. Kathy remembered that her grandmother arrived for visits carrying blue Samsonite luggage and smelling of Ben-Gay, but she couldn't remember anything her grandmother ever said.

John's Cherokee grandmother taught him basic courtesy: "When you go to someone's house, don't ask for anything and accept everything that is offered."

Sasha's Russian babushka told him, "You have right to go anywhere." What did that mean in the Soviet Union in the 1980s? Was she giving him wings of freedom? Courage in society?

Other grandmothers' advice was like something out of a mystery novel. Diane's Oklahoma grandmother said, "A whistling woman is up to no good." And still plainer, Hilary's Scots grandmother told her, "Don't sit too close to the fire." That made sense when I learned that it was so cold in her grandmother's stone house in Scotland, Hilary *had* just been sitting too close to the fireplace and had set her cape on fire.

Often our grandmothers taught us basic rules of life, didn't they? That we need to occupy ourselves, to respect others, to be polite, to be independent. One grandmother was impatient with a bored grandchild. "If you can't entertain yourself," she said, "don't expect someone else to entertain you." And another advised adventurousness: "Breakfast in Oklahoma, dinner in Texas," she said.

Some of the advice I heard about was as practical as a hammer. When Teresa said she was so stressed about her career that she was about to crack up, her grandmother said, "Honey, you can't afford a nervous breakdown. You don't have any money. You have to get a job first."

In our youthful dramas, our grandmothers could be rocks of sensibility. One woman called in tears to tell her grandmother about the dramatic end of a college romance. The boyfriend had asked her to marry him and she said no and now he was in such despair and so upset that she thought he might kill himself. She cried. Her grandmother listened and then said, "So he thinks you're the last potato on the plate, does he?" The air went out of the drama. Everybody lived happily.

Some people would not even consider proposing their grandmothers as good examples. "Oh, you don't want any advice from my grandmother," Sandy told me. "She was a pistol. She had four husbands and never bothered with legalities and paperwork any of the four times."

So much for classic stereotypes of saintly, silver-haired grandmothers. Now that I am a step-grandmother and a godmother and a great-aunt, I want to be remembered for my poetic wise words. There is, though, that nagging thought that at least one person thinks of me as a four-and-a-half-pound hen with a fancy topknot of feathers. That sort of takes the edge off of a wise woman.

August 10 Is Lazy Day

Swimsuits and Chocolate

Never, ever come to Oklahoma in August, even if somebody begs you.

It is miserably hot. Thanks to all the lakes we have built, the humidity is so high that it feels as if a big dog were breathing on us all day.

Furthermore, in Oklahoma, August lasts two months. The second half, we call September. We crawl around like lizards, flicking out our tongues in vicious oaths and heartfelt vows that next year we will spend the month somewhere else.

Late September can find us getting the worst sunburn of the year at the OU–Texas game. That is in Dallas, granted, and usually in October, but we still sharpen the grievance against the heat to a fine point.

Emily Dickinson wrote about a summer that "Bestirred itself—put on its Coat," and we take that literally. Much like deluded missionaries in James Michener's *Hawaii*, when the calendar says September, we believe it. We put away our beige shoes and put on brown shoes. We begin wearing long sleeves, stockings, and dark colors. We are slaves to the calendar. In August we decide that it is time for school to start, and we send the children to classrooms with no air conditioning.

In my summer garden, just about the only things still holding up their heads are zinnias. I love zinnias for their hardiness and color. I am quite fond of a new green zinnia with the name of "Envy."

Do not sell envy short. I have learned that envy is a very useful sin. Envy is a signal that something is missing in my life—usually a dream I have abandoned. I cultivate the longing until it propels me to action. This is much like blowing on an ember until it bursts into flame. C. S. Lewis wrote that pain is what drives us out of the nursery room and into the real world. Mr. Hedley told us students that pain tells us we are alive; we pinch ourselves to see if we are awake. If I were mixing up a concoction for happiness, I would stir in a pinch of envy and a dash of pain—not too much, just enough for an interesting taste.

Artisan chocolatiers add cayenne pepper to their chocolate for a complex taste. Remember the movie *Chocolat* and how Juliette Binoche added cayenne pepper to her hot chocolate drink? The Aztec emperor Montezuma drank his spicy cacao from a golden vessel. It was the drink for warriors, nobles, and traders.

August is like that—a golden vessel with some heat. The spicy surprise is the sudden cloudburst with hammering rain. For lowering the temperature, these are about as effective as a child's temper tantrum in public. All they do is make us peevish.

It was August that got me entangled in some bad shopping.

I have always wanted a movie star figure, and at last I have one. Unfortunately, the movie star is SpongeBob SquarePants.

You know those times you find yourself doing something you never, ever thought you would do? That is what happened to me. After years of being a happy landlubber, I found myself shopping for a swimsuit. I agreed to go to a pool party with some women friends. Although water and swimsuits were involved, I convinced myself that it would be like the old country-western song, "I Fell in with Evil Companions, Now I'm Having the Time of My Life."

If there is anything more humbling than shopping for a swimsuit, I don't want to know what it is.

First, I went to the size I used to wear. After a quick trip to the fitting room, I moved smartly to the rack containing the size I thought I could wear. Then on to the rack of the size I thought I ought to wear. Finally, beaten down and disheartened, shuffling along like an actor in an old prison movie, I went to the rack of suits that I can wear.

At first, the clerks were cheery and helpful. They called to me through the dressing room door in chirpy voices, offering to fetch different styles, colors, or, they said in hushed tones, different sizes. I made so many trips back and forth to the racks carrying armloads of swimsuits that they eventually abandoned hope. I was reminded of a sailor recounting the sinking of his ship. "And then I heard the captain say," he said, "'Save yourself.'"

On I trudged. The clerks had lost both interest and their cheery tones. They leaned on the counter, talking among themselves. Once in a while, they would gesture me toward racks. A flip of the hand told me, "Big sizes—that-a way."

Since this was August and swimsuits had been on sale since June, selections were limited. I ended up with a green-and-turquoise two-piece thing that makes me resemble a beach ball. Why, oh why did we ever do away with bathing costumes? Those big, black knitted things with skirts that came to the knees.

Dispirited, I came home vowing to lose fifteen pounds. I have a tummy I never had before and a roll around my middle as if I'm wearing a fanny pack backwards. According to an article in *USA Today*, abdominal fat is the most dangerous fat. "This fat isn't a static cluster of useless tissue," wrote David Zinczenko, author of *The Abs Diet* book. "It's a living, growing mass, practically an organism all its own, one that builds, divides, and excretes toxins back into our system, that draws blood flow and nutrients away from the rest of our bodies, that alters the distribution of hormones in our bloodstreams, that presses on our organs and hampers their function." I don't know which is worse, that image of abdominal fat or the bloated fifty-three-word sentence describing it.

I taped "Diet" on every mirror in the house. I swore that I would eat nothing white. I would drink nothing alcoholic or carbonated. I would resume my morning stretches and exercises. I would add a sit-up or two. Once in a while. Better still, I would get back to the gym.

What I like best about the gym is walking on the treadmill and watching *Biography* on A&E, despite my close call with this activity: once I fell off the treadmill while trying to get a closer look at Patrick Swayze. I promised myself that I would add the rowing machine, the bicycle, and the weight machine. I would pump iron until I had abs of steel. In my golden years, I might even tan until I turned bronze. I was giddy with metallic metaphors.

About this time, I was passing by the clothing department on another shopping adventure when I caught sight of a rack of silky black pants. Perfect. I have been wanting silky black pants. These were rayon, not silk, but seemed fine. Very reasonably priced. And best yet, size Small fit perfectly. A bit long, but still—Small. Maybe I have been wrong about that fifteen pounds. Maybe I have worried it off. Wished it off. Willed it off. Oh happy day, size Small.

When I got home with my happy pants and looked at them more closely, I discovered that they are maternity pants. I had hit bottom.

Then I read the book *Brenda's Wardrobe Companion* by Brenda Kinsel. I read this book as if I'd discovered the Holy Grail. For me, Brenda's wardrobe book has two major parts. The Old Testament is how to get dressed, and the New Testament is how to clean out and organize your closet. Now, these are subjects you would think that I would have learned by now. I am what the French diplomatically call "a woman of a certain age." I like that phrase—it has allure.

Brenda tells us to ruthlessly get rid of all the clothes in our closet that have expired. She means expired as in out-of-date dairy products.

Her advice: Get rid of everything we bought to wear when we lose ten pounds, that we have not worn in a year or so, that is out of style, and that does not make us feel good no matter how much it cost or what a good bargain it was. Most of all, get rid of anything that does not fit.

The book's subtitle is revealing: *A Guide to Getting Dressed from the Inside Out.* It guides us through figuring out what image we want: romantic, dramatic, professional. What clothes make us feel good, what colors we like now.

Buy only what we love—from tissues to umbrellas, but especially clothes. Lingerie, sleepwear, casual clothes, clothes for work, garden, or social events—do not wear "just okay" stuff; wear only the clothes we love, because this is about loving ourselves.

People change. Maybe we used to like pastels; now we like hot salsa colors. Used to like to dress in froufrou clothes; now we want to look tailored. And most of all, our bodies change with age, health, medication, lifestyle.

Brenda's rule is to dress the body you have now and love the body you have. Don't refuse to buy clothes until you lose twenty pounds or get back to a size eight. The book's fundamental rule: Make sure the clothes fit. Pay attention to fit, not to size.

In August I am ready to hear this. Summer has dragged on too long. I am tired of the heat and the weeds in my garden and my clothes and my girth. Tired of trying to lose fifteen pounds. Tired of fussing about it.

One of the few bright spots in my garden in late summer and early autumn is the appearance of hummingbirds. My garden is jeweled with emerald hummingbirds energetically visiting the ruby hibiscus flaunting their hardiness and the last of the ragged hollyhocks. I watched out the window as one energetic little hummingbird zipped from flower to flower and then—what a surprise—landed on a tree branch to rest for a minute. I have never seen a hummingbird at rest, taking a tiny load off. Maybe that is what I need to do: sit down for a minute and wait for the seasons to change.

I was doing just that when the phone rang with an invitation I could not dream up in my fattest, jolliest fantasies. I was asked to judge a nonprofit organization's chocolate contest. Eat chocolate for a good cause.

Thank you, Jesus. And Brenda.

August 15 Is National Failures Day

How Did I Get into This Mess?

Few things in my life have begun with such high hopes and foundered on such despair as home renovation projects. The only thing saving them from total failure has been more time and more money—both mine.

You want to talk home renovation? I could tell you stories that make men wince and women grow steely eyed with empathetic vengeance.

Neither of those responses helps. I know because I have tried it both ways. I have cried and cursed and sued and begged and refused to get out of bed. "Let them hammer and saw and paint around us," I said to the cat as we pulled the cover over our heads. "Let them sand the sheetrock until plaster dust settles over us like the scene from *Sleeping Beauty.*"

That doesn't help either. Eventually, I had to get out of bed, learn how many shades of white ceiling paint exist, and then go fetch some for the painter.

Things I didn't know when I began:

1. Even if the contractor is a neighbor he can still be a snake.
2. You can't believe how fast you can be cheated out of $30,000.
3. According to the district attorney's office, an abandoned hole in the ground that was supposed to be a room does not prove "intent to defraud."
4. I didn't know workers arrived so early and stayed so late.
5. I didn't know I was going to have to be the foreman on the job.
6. When the telephone man looks at the string attached to the buried cable and asks, "What's this?"—it's trouble.

7. When the electrician's able-bodied son is lying prostrate on the grass—things aren't going well.
8. Asking a yard full of workers, "Does anyone know why the electricity went off in the house?" doesn't elicit an answer you want to hear.
9. When a repairman says, "This'll just take about fifteen minutes" —there goes half a day.
10. When the plumber says, "Uh-oh,"—you don't want to know why.
11. When someone says, "In six months you won't even notice this"—try not to overreact.
12. When the contractor looks at the architectural renderings and says, "Well, if it were me, I would . . ."—it's best not to repeat that suggestion to the architect.
13. The contractor does not have to know everything the architect says about him.
14. When it is all over and the roof leaks and the door won't open, architects and honest contractors don't understand hysterical midnight phone calls. They shrug and refer to this as "bugs to be worked out."
15. Believe it or not, the bugs do get worked out.

This project was one long rendition of "Oh Woeful Me, I've Got Those Home Renovation Blues"—with about a hundred verses. Most of the time I am entangled in small home improvement jobs with my sidekick Tony.

Tony will cheerfully tackle anything—yard work, furniture repairs, and minor construction. Lack of experience doesn't hold him back. He is Asian and isn't able to read English well (as in instructions, directions, and warnings), but that does not deter him. He is eager, industrious, hardworking, scrupulously honest, and delighted with any project we undertake.

When we built a picket fence, he sunk the fence posts and had pickets halfway across the front yard when some smarty-pants told us we were building on a city right-of-way. So Tony dug up the posts and moved the fence. The fence stretched across the front of the lawn when I noticed that half the pickets stood above the sloping ground like high-water pants. Tony proposed hauling in dirt to raise the ground to meet the pickets, but I went to the bookstore and bought a book: *How to Build a Fence.* I read it and showed the pictures to Tony. Together we learned how to build a fence so that it followed the roll of the land. But first, we had to take down the fence. Again. A neighbor drove by and yelled, "Why don't you put it on wheels? Then you can move it wherever you want it."

Now we are installing vinyl floor tiles in the garage quarters. Did you know there are directions that tell you how to keep the lines of the tile from serpentining across the floor?

For our next project, I am going to read the directions first.

August 26 (1920) Is a Day of Women's Suffrage*

Wise Women and Rabbits

Maybe it is because I was close to my grandmother, but I have always had older women in my life, long before I heard the word "mentor." They have been teachers, writers, churchwomen, musicians, landladies, and mothers—ordinary heroines who keep society humming smoothly. They are women who know how to do things—serve tea, make a salmon loaf, crochet, make a career, grow a family. They have had adventures, disasters, revelations, and interesting lives—been a nurse in World War II, lived through the 1930s Depression, had psychic experiences. One was taught to play the harp by the same person who taught Harpo Marx. One, a priest, experienced the death by suicide of two of her children. She was almost eighty years old when she had a hip replacement so she could process into the church to become the first female Episcopal priest in Oklahoma in 1978.

I love these older women. Their homes were places of respite—little domestic oases that felt like sinking into a great, soft pillow. We talked. They listened and they said important things or they just nodded in understanding. They had a gift for asking hard questions. Jean, the older woman who was a harpist and my spiritual advisor, changed my life when she asked of my husband, "Is he the one true love of your life?"

So I was alarmed to look up one day and see that many of them have disappeared from my life—they are frail or relocated or dead. That

* The 19th Amendment to the U.S. Constitution granted women the right to vote. The amendment was passed by Congress on June 14, 1919, and was ratified by three-fourths of the states on August 18, 1920. The secretary of state certified the ratification on August 26, 1920.

means I am no longer the young woman sitting at their feet. And then I realized—I am the wise older woman. Or should be. It is my turn to pour tea for young women and to tell them where I have been and to talk to them about where they are going. And frankly, I don't know if I am up to the task.

Sometimes I think I have plenty of wisdom to share; other times I wonder who wants to know what it was like to wear Yardley cologne and a miniskirt in the 1970s. Oh dear, am I letting down my gender?

Then I remembered one season when I was working for a ballet company and all during the *Nutcracker* performances the children cast as bunnies kept fouling up the choreography of the great battle scene. The bunnies were so excited that they hopped in front of the cannon, which meant it could not be fired. That eliminated the great crescendo boom when the Mouse King is killed. Instead of a dramatic finale, he just sank to the floor quietly. Dead. The bunnies were corrected repeatedly, but still they hopped to the wrong spot. The stage manager was furious and said in his Southern accent, "I told those rabbits myself, stay out of the line of fire."

Now I am ready. Any young woman who comes calling and wants to talk about life, mine and hers, and secrets of the universe, I will tell her this: "Little rabbit, in the great ballet of life, when you get to the battle scene, do not stand in front of the cannon. More tea?"

August Is Romance Awareness Month

Cowgirl Punch

Romance wears many costumes. One of the most unappreciated romantic figures is the cowgirl. Not just the famous ones such as Annie Oakley, or the notorious ones like Belle Starr, but the skilled horsewomen from the performers of the 101 Ranch Show to rodeo's current barrel-racing champions.

My friend Jeanne is a horsewoman from Wyoming—a strong, independent, capable woman. When she moved to Oklahoma, she was amazed to find that Oklahoma women like being identified by their married names—Mrs. Brown and Mrs. James. She thinks of us Oklahoma women as Southern belles, just a little soft and fluffy for her taste.

When I first met her, Jeanne was the director of a library and indefatigable—up at dawn to feed the horses before setting out in stockings and heels for an eight-hour day at the office, then home to train the horses and muck out the stalls. Lights out about midnight.

Now she has realized her dream of training horses full time, but she not only trains horses, she trains people to train horses. The walls of her ranch library are dripping with ribbons, awards, and photos of prizewinning horses. With that outdoors image of her, I have been surprised by her new interest—she has been e-mailing holiday recipes to her friends.

This is her recipe.

Cowgirl Punch

16 ounces cranberry juice cocktail
1 small can frozen limeade
1 small can bourbon

Mix together and freeze for a few days. Recipe can be tripled easily.

I have shared the recipe with other strong women. My sister does not drink, but she said that recipes are meant to be tinkered with and I should experiment with this one. Substituting, perhaps, vodka for the bourbon. And making a double batch. Jeanne and I like that idea.

My journalist training makes me snoopy, so as we were getting acquainted, I asked Jeanne about the multiple photos of one horse. Clearly there was something special about the mare, an award-winning quarter horse mare registered as Karen Clegg but called Dee. Indeed there was. Jeanne told me the story of how she had raised and trained Dee from a colt; how they competed in reining contests, a demanding test of skill with Jeanne the only woman competing against men; how she and Dee won only top prizes at every competition they entered, and how all her professional horsemen friends agreed—Dee was destined to be the undefeated national champion.

When Jeanne fell in love with an Oklahoma man, she said that she would relocate only if they had land for her horses. He immediately bought a ranch. Jeanne was driving alone, trucking Dee from Wyoming to her new home, when it looked like rain. She stopped at a roadside rest stop and let Dee out to stretch her legs and eat a bite or two of grass. That is what the mare was doing when a freak lightning bolt killed her instantly. Jeanne said she could not even talk about the incident for seven years.

She told me this story as only one can tell of a true heartbreak, matter-of-factly. As she talked, I could see the scene as she must have seen it—against a darkening prairie sky, the silhouette of the beautiful horse sunk to her knees in death, her head thrown back, and still tethered to the horse trailer.

A couple of brawny truckers were at the rest stop, and Jeanne asked them to help load her horse into the trailer. "Lady," they told her, "there's no way. This horse must weigh almost a thousand pounds."

Jeanne summoned her Wyoming steel and told them, "I'm loading her." And they did.

She drove on to Oklahoma in the rain, alone and crying all the way. She cried herself dry and then she threw up the rest of the way. "It was a heavy load," she told me. "It still is."

The next holiday, I'm going to make Jeanne's recipe for cowgirl punch, and I'll think of Jeanne every time I serve it. She closed her recipe e-mail to me with a couple of lines of poem by an anonymous poet. I don't know who wrote it, but I like it:

She never shook the stars
from their appointed courses,
But she loved good men,
and she rode good horses.

September

Autumn begins to be inferred
By millinery of the cloud
Or deeper color in the shawl
That wraps the everlasting hill.

—Emily Dickinson, from poem 1682

September Begins the Peak of Cold Season

Belief and the Common Cold

Never underestimate the power of the common cold.

Or the power of belief.

When I was in journalism school, I took classes in propaganda and psychological warfare and in advertising—all much the same—and that's when I learned that truth is not a factor necessary to belief.

Sometimes we believe things that are not true. We believe what we want to believe. We believe that the right toothpaste or hair product will make us so alluring that we will attract our dream mate and that person will make us happy forever after.

This may not be true, but we believe it and it sells lots of toothpaste and hair products.

We also believe that over-the-counter remedies and home cures will alleviate the common cold. I have been believing that a lot lately, ever since I caught a heavy cold.

I know the folk wisdom about a cold—that it's three days coming, three days with you, and three days going and there's not much we can do to shorten the cycle.

On Day One, however, I was so miserable that I rushed to the grocery store determined to try every remedy I could think of.

I bought cans of chicken soup—the classic remedy. And ground beef for chili because I heard that spicy food helps a cold.

"How you doing?" asked the friendly butcher.

"Terrible," I sniffled. "I've got a cold."

"What you need for that," volunteered the strangers standing beside me, "is fresh ginger. Brewed in hot, herbal tea—preferably echinacea tea."

I raced to the produce counter, where I had intended to go anyway to buy grapefruits and oranges. "Make a juice that's half grapefruit and half orange juice," someone told me. "It's that combination that will cure a cold."

"For my cold," I told another shopper, holding up my fresh ginger with one hand and wiping my nose with a paper towel in the other hand. I was long past mere tissues. Day One and I was already into Bounty paper towels.

"Ginger will cure the symptoms," the couple told me, "but it's raw garlic that will cure the cold." The woman nodded sagely as the man went on to explain, "Slice the garlic very thin and eat it with cheese on crackers. Now when you first bite it, it will burn your mouth, and then your breath will smell bad . . ."

He went on with his tutorial, and I thought, "This is what it's like to have a cold. People think only dolts get colds, so they stand you up in public and tell you what garlic tastes like."

I bought zinc lozenges, cough suppressants, expectorants, decongestant sprays, and homeopathic cold tablets. I had fresh fruit and pots of hot tea.

My favorite remedy, however, was megadoses of vitamin C washed down with champagne. This is supposed to get the vitamin C into the blood system quicker. After two or three doses of this, I didn't mind the cold so much. I lay on the sofa and dozed through old movies, feeling sorry for myself.

You have noticed, of course, that trouble comes in bundles, so while I was on my sickbed, lights burned out, batteries went dead, garage door openers wouldn't work, I broke dishes and cut my hand on the shards, and something got stuck in the vacuum cleaner.

Two weeks of this hell and damnation, and then I was well. I replaced the light bulbs and dead batteries and dismantled the vacuum cleaner to discover—what a surprise—that a cat toy had clogged it up.

Everything is in working order now, myself included. It was the vitamin C and champagne that cured me. I really believe that. Never underestimate the power of belief.

These classic recipes are from the classic cookbook *Food and Cookery for the Sick and Convalescent,* by Fannie M. Farmer (Boston: Little, Brown, 1911).

Chicken Broth

3 ½ pounds chicken
2 tablespoons rice
3 pints cold water
1 ½ teaspoons salt
Few grains pepper

Clean chicken; remove skin and fat, disjoint, and wipe with a wet cloth. Put in kettle, add cold water, heat slowly until boiling, skim, and cook until meat is tender. Add salt and pepper when half cooked, then strain, and remove fat. Reheat to boiling, add rice, and cook until rice is soft. It is sometimes necessary to cook rice separately and rub through a sieve before adding to broth.

Chicken Broth with Egg

Beat one egg slightly and pour in gradually while stirring constantly one cup hot chicken stock. Cook one minute and strain. Care must be taken that egg does not become overcooked, as broth would have a curdled appearance.

September 1 Is Unofficial
Know When to Fold 'Em Day

Poker and Me

This is not an authentic holiday. I made up this holiday because I want to talk about the only world champion gambler I ever met—Bobby Baldwin.

I don't know if I am very, very au courant or have been around so long that I am retro.

Take poker. It has become what the press calls "a mainstream obsession." Online poker. Poker clinics. Poker tournaments. Celebrity poker players. Some six thousand contestants compete annually at the World Series of Poker in Las Vegas.

Hang on to your chips, because we are in the eye of poker mania. The *New York Times* has hired a poker columnist and is full of stories these days about poker champions such as Stu "Stuey the Kid" Unger and the vegetarian card stud Daniel Negreanu.

But while these people were still toddlers, I knew world champion poker player Bobby Baldwin, and I invited him to the University of Tulsa to teach a class. He did. He taught a continuing education class titled "Bobby Baldwin's Winning Poker Secrets." *Gambling Times* magazine ran an article about the class.

I am not surprised that the American Indian casinos in Oklahoma are making more money than they can haul away in trucks. Of all the continuing education classes I presented at TU's College of Arts and Sciences, the two most popular were Bobby Baldwin's poker class and classes on handicapping horse races with the track announcer from Oaklawn Park. People drove for hours through a snowstorm to attend the handicapping classes.

It was not hard to meet Bobby Baldwin then. He lived in Tulsa. His family lived in Tulsa. His twin brother was a landscape gardener.

The people who signed up for Bobby's poker class told me one after another that he was the most courteous person they had ever met. They all commented on his good manners. Ah, yes, riverboat gambler charm.

And here is how we returned the favor. During his class, tornado sirens went off and campus security evacuated us all into the hall until the all-clear sounded. While we were out there, hiding for our lives, someone stole a hundred-dollar poker book that Bobby had brought with him.

When I knew him in 1979, Bobby was twenty-eight years old and the youngest professional poker player on the circuit. He was on his way to Las Vegas to defend his title at the World Series of Poker. He told me, "I know how Billy the Kid felt."

He looked up from that game in Las Vegas and saw me standing with the other spectators looking at him over a golden rope. He had just seen me a couple days earlier in Tulsa and I never mentioned a trip to Las Vegas because the trip was not planned. I had an unexpected invitation on a private plane. Most of us would have been startled or surprised. He didn't bat an eye, did nothing more than glance at me, and went back to his game. Talk about a poker face. When he took a break, he came over to greet me and my husband.

At home in Tulsa, he was a quiet family man with flash. He carried his poker chips in a Halston case and wore a diamond as big as a Ritz cracker. He drove a black Lincoln Mark V with a license plate that said "HOLD EM" and his wife drove a yellow Mark V with the word "POKER" on the plate. They had a blue Mark V, an extra, with an ordinary plate. "I like fancy cars," he said, "fine cars and expensive houses. It's part of the dream."

The only game he played while home was golf, and that was for relaxation. "I don't even like to see cards when I'm home," he said. "It would be like a postman taking a walk." Sometimes the Life Master bridge player played tournament bridge but only for recreation, never for money. For Bobby, playing cards for money isn't play.

He lived in Tulsa then, but he made his money on the road, playing the pro circuit in Texas, Kentucky, Nevada, Louisiana, Colorado, and Arkansas—never in Oklahoma. The height of poker season then was football's off-season, and Bobby was out of town for a dozen games a month. Games dragged on for hours, days, or weeks. The threat of hijackings and kidnappings was ever present. At home, he and his family were protected by the best security system he could find.

Bobby discovered poker when he was twelve years old. He began his poker education by losing six dollars. That loss taught him to respect the game, he said, "because it deceives weak players into believing it's a game of luck when it is primarily a game of skill."

By high school, he had also discovered pool, which kept him in pocket money and earned him the nickname "Fast Bobby" for his speedy shots. He became a world-class billiards player. In Tulsa, he was King of Cue City with his fast moves and sure shots, but he never hustled a game. Poker and pool put him through Oklahoma State University with a major in business administration. He scheduled his classes around regular poker games.

In 1970, he took his winnings—$5,000 stuffed into a Kleenex box—and went to Las Vegas for a vacation. He lost it all, everything but three $25 chips. Then he got hot. He was a young King Midas and everything he touched turned green. He played blackjack and won. He played baccarat and won. Casino guards had to hold back the crowds. One man was allowed to meet the kid on a hot streak; his name was Arnold Palmer. By morning, Bobby had won $180,000. He took it home in a dress box. A plainclothes guard with a .45 went with him. That is when he decided to become a professional gambler. He was nineteen.

He treated himself to an expensive set of poker chips with his initials engraved on them. Three months later he had lost it all, including the poker chips, but he bounced back big.

He went on to win four titles, including Seven Card Stud World Champion in 1977, World Champion Poker Player in 1978, Superbowl of Poker Champions in 1979, No Limit Deuce-to-Seven Lowball World Champion 1977, and more. He excelled at Hold 'Em, which is a variation of seven card stud.

In Hold 'Em, each player gets two cards down and plays the board with the five community cards on the table. "It sounds simple," Bobby told me, "but there are one thousand, three hundred and eighty two-card holdings you can have." Hold 'Em is poker's most precise game, he said, and he considered it more exciting and more intriguing than other games.

Not long after that, Bobby left Tulsa and moved to Las Vegas. He went to work for the Golden Nugget Casino; in 1978 he became head of the Mirage; in 1998 was named president of the Bellagio Hotel and Casino; and in 2000 became the chief executive officer of the Mirage Resorts subsidiary of MGM Mirage. In 2003, he was inducted into the Poker Hall of Fame. The casino executive still plays high-stakes poker and has written a couple of books about the game.

His standard of ethics and his immeasurable talent have brought him not only success but also the admiration of his gambling peers.

"Baldwin is the Tom Watson of poker players," one said, "clean-cut and honorable."

Professionally, he is known for his aggressive poker philosophy. "Winning is your motive," he said. "Never play anyone soft." That is his melody. The harmony is his respectful gambler's creed: "Honor the game. It's an art form."

"Betting that kid is like trying to take a banana away from a gorilla," Amarillo Slim said.

"He's super aggressive," Doyle Brunson said, "but a true Southern gentleman."

The *Chicago Sun Times,* covering the 1978 championship playoff, described him as "clever, daring, and, like all good card players, cold blooded."

Some of the players called him "The Owl" then because of the way he scrutinized his opponents with wise eyes. "There's more psychology than math involved in poker," he said. "I don't play the cards; I play the player." His winning formula is a combination of natural talent and personal character.

"The personal gambling creed I live by," he told me, "is never misrepresent yourself. Honor is everything to a gambler. Establish a reputation for always paying your debts, never cheating, and never hustling."

Football Season Begins

You Know Who I Mean

I am all for politically correct. Really, really for it.

Oh, I like blonde jokes, but I am blonde, so I think that's okay.

Naturally, I am all over the issue of American Indian nicknames for sports teams.

In the last year or so, the NCAA has been noodling around with the thorny issue of colleges and universities with mascots named Braves, Red Men, and Savages. Will the Indian imagery be banned altogether? Derided as racist and demeaning?

This could affect some thirty schools with names such as Warriors, Indians, Choctaws, Seminoles, Aztecs, Utes, Chippewas, and Fighting Sioux. With the first action by the NCAA, chiefs of Oklahoma tribes praised efforts to eliminate the use of Indian names for mascots, decrying the terms as "hostile, abusive, derogatory, hateful and disrespectful."

In Florida, however, Florida State University officials called the NCAA action "outrageous and insulting" and said that they intended to hang on to their mascot name. What's more, Seminole tribal leaders supported the university in this determination. FSU's mascot name and symbols proudly refer to the "unconquered" spirit of the Seminole Tribe of Florida, the university president said.

I am feeling pretty smug that my own alma maters have more politically correct names: Coffeyville College has the Red Ravens, and the University of Tulsa has the Golden Hurricane.

But wait, are we also being insensitive to the animal world when we allow athletic teams to name themselves Bearcats and Bengals? Should we reconsider the Anteaters at the University of California–Irvine, the Antelopes at the University of Nebraska–Kearney, and colleges with nicknames such as Badgers, Bald Eagles, and Banana Slugs? What about the Bantams, Bears, Beavers, and Bees? Will we say so long to Bison, Blood Hounds, and Black Flies? Will it be farewell to Blue Jays, Bobcats, Bulldogs, Camels, Coyotes, Cougars, Ducks, Dolphins, and Eagles? Will we lose the Razorbacks, the Squirrels, the Spiders, and the Stags? A college in New York has a team called the Turtles, and a university in Maryland calls its team the Terrapins, neither of which summons an image of offense or speed to me.

We do not have space to go through the entire alphabet, but suffice to say that the list extends through Wildcats, Wolves, Yellow Jackets, and the White Mules of Colby College in Maine.

What would that leave us? The names of human behavior and character traits seem acceptable. We already have the Vandals, the Valiants, and the Saints. But there are the Claim Jumpers of Conway, Arkansas; and dare we mention the Sooners of the University of Oklahoma? I am also part Irish and wonder if I should be offended that Notre Dame's team is the Fighting Irish.

Ethnicity is not off-limits, because we have the Celts, the Britons, and the Scots. Some teams have the nicknames of professions—Archers, Cowboys, Prophets, Professors, Presidents, and Statesmen. Whittier College in California refers to its team as the Poets. For religion, there are three Quakers, two Preachers, one Praying Colonels, and a Parsons. The Crusaders, alas, have been protested, as being anti-Muslim. Two teams are named the Vulcans, from Roman mythology, after the god of fire. Six teams are called the Titans, after giants in Greek mythology.

A few teams are named for acts of nature—the Pepperdine Waves, the Tornado of King College in Tennessee, the Nor'Easters in Maine, the Northern Lights in Montana, the Lake Erie College Storm, and the University of Hawaii's Rainbows.

At least three teams have the name of a noun, including the Bridges of Brooklyn College and the Lamps of a Baptist seminary in Tennessee. I am fond of the Ramblin' Wreck of Georgia Tech because it is fun to say. The name dates back to the 1920s, when the young engineers constructed makeshift mechanical buggies. Tech's fight song is so popular, Vice President Richard Nixon and Nikita Khrushchev sang it at their historic Moscow meeting in 1959.

And then there are what I classify as just plain weird names. These include, in Ohio, Heidelberg College's Student Princes, along with the

Trolls of Trinity Christian College in Illinois and the New York University Violets. In Pennsylvania, Rosemont College cheers for the Rosemonsters. The baseball team at California State University in Long Beach, California, is known as the Dirtbags.

Maybe the safest thing would be to have no nicknames or mascots for the teams. Perhaps that would make us fans kinder and gentler folks. Then we could just shout,

> Romp 'em, stomp 'em,
> Bim, bam, boo.
> Go, go, go—You Know Who.

The Last Week of September
Is Banned Book Week

ABCs of Obscenity

Oh no.

I heard a fragment of a story on National Public Radio about some-one wanting to ban *To Kill a Mockingbird* because it is racially offensive.

Well, that's the point of the book, isn't it? Alabama in the 1930s was racially offensive.

So I looked up "All Things Considered" on the Internet, and oh no, the whole story was worse than I thought. The Chicago Public Library has chosen Harper Lee's novel for its "One City, One Book" program. *To Kill a Mockingbird* is the American classic that has sold 15 million copies and won the Pulitzer Prize. The organization complaining about the book is—here it comes—Muskogee High School, which has taken the book off its freshmen's required reading list because some people were offended by it. Muskogee is in Oklahoma.

Great. Our state takes another giant step backward in the eyes of the world. Reminds everyone that our public education denies, denounces —yea, even damns—the philosophy of evolution. Why don't we go out to the Port of Catoosa and erect a statue of a woman holding a torch with the flame extinguished? And bearing a plaque that reads, "Give me your ignorant, your close minded, your uneducated masses yearning to stay in the dark."

Not that I don't think we should both debate and champion books. But as I see it, this is not just about freedom of speech or censorship. It is about common sense. Do we have to see everything from the vantage point of revisionist history?

Times change. Sensibilities change. Language changes. People, we hope to heaven, change as we struggle toward enlightenment. Then we can look back and see how ignorant and quaint we were.

I grew up in Nowata, a little town in northeastern Oklahoma that did not have a public library when I was a girl. The public school had a library, but it was closed in the summer. The first books I remember reading were from the school library's lower shelves, the books for elementary grades. I read biographies of Sacagawea and Lou Gehrig. It was such a magical experience that I proceeded to read all the books on the lower shelves and then all of them on the intermediate shelves. I read them as fast as I could.

And then, oh happy day, Mrs. Lucille Gillespie started a little lending library in her front hall. She was as short and stout as a hen, the energetic advisor of the Rainbow Girls organization, and a good soul. But to me, Mrs. Gillespie earned stars in her crown in heaven for a few shelves of books she opened to me. I could go up the street and down an alley, walk into her hall, and take out any book I wanted.

I am saddened to see good things like books and libraries be scourged by small minds and large mouths.

The books most frequently banned or challenged in schools and public libraries between 1990 and 1992 include not only *Catcher in the Rye, The Adventures of Tom Sawyer,* and *The Adventures of Huckleberry Finn* (which are regularly hauled out and beaten up) but also these sizzlers: *A Wrinkle in Time* by Madeleine L'Engle, *Blubber* by Judy Blume, *I Know Why the Caged Bird Sings* by Maya Angelou, *The Color Purple* by Alice Walker, *The Grapes of Wrath* by John Steinbeck, *James and the Giant Peach* by Roald Dahl, and *Little Red Ridinghood* as told by the Grimm brothers.

Other books that have been barred, banned, and/or seized through history include *Ulysses, Candide, Canterbury Tales, Moll Flanders,* and various editions of *The Arabian Nights.* The publisher of Margaret Sanger's book about contraception was jailed; Boston authorities threatened criminal prosecution because of the explicit language in Walt Whitman's *Leaves of Grass.*

Around the world, Jack London's *Call of the Wild* was censored in European dictatorships; Mary Shelley's *Frankenstein* was banned in apartheid South Africa, along with the classic book about a horse titled *Black Beauty.* The Soviet Union banned the Bible from importation for thirty years. In 1999 a teacher—mercifully not in Oklahoma this time but in Georgia—required students to have permission slips before they could read three titillating works of sex, violence, and adult language. Those works were *Hamlet, MacBeth,* and *King Lear.* In the 1980s, *The Merchant of Venice* was banned from Michigan classrooms because of its portrayal of the Jewish character Shylock. And in 1996, New Hampshire schools pulled a book from the curriculum because the romance of a young woman disguised as a boy violated a "prohibition of alternative lifestyle instruction"; that was Shakespeare's play *Twelfth Night.*

Recently, the pope criticized the Harry Potter books, I heard an Episcopal bishop preach a sermon damning the kid's movie *Harriet the Spy,* and I understand that the J.R.R. Tolkien books have been removed from the bookstore at Oral Roberts University.

Censorship is a slippery slope. Humorist Jean Kerr had another spin. "I know a man who says the waters of the world are gathered in the armpit of an old Indian," she said. "I don't know that I would defend to the death his right to say that."

The American Library Association designates the last week in September as Banned Books Week to celebrate the freedom to read. In observation of that, I am going to read something naughty, something that has made the hit list. Maybe Charles Darwin's *On the Origin of Species* or maybe *How to Eat Fried Worms* by Thomas Rockwell.

Maybe I'll flout authority and read both of them. Let 'em come get me. They'll never take me alive.

September Is National Courtesy Month

Mind Your Manners

I

Every detail about this story is important.

The setting: It was during the winter holidays. A cold day. I was downtown. Old-fashioned cosmopolitan setting. Hurrying along the street I met Robert LaFortune, former mayor of the city and an elderly gentleman. He looked quite dapper and proper in a topcoat, scarf, and hat.

"Hello, Mr. LaFortune," I said.

"Well, Connie," he replied—tipping his hat—"How do you do. Happy holidays."

Tipping his hat. How long has it been since a man politely tipped his hat at me?

I was thrilled with the gallant gesture.

I am not picketing for a return to the corsetted 1950s. I am not rejecting feminism. It was just a wonderful simple feeling of courtesy, manners, custom. Ritual at its finest.

I believe that how we dress affects not only the way people respond to us but also how we perceive ourselves and how we perform.

I believe the same thing about the little courtesies.

The grand radio and television broadcaster Eric Sevareid was once asked about his technique of interviewing. "You ask the most personal, probing questions," he was told, "and yet people answer you. What is your secret?"

Mr. Sevareid replied, "It's an old-fashioned technique—called courtesy."

A tip of the hat, an opening of the door, pulling out a chair, standing when a woman enters the room, standing when anyone enters, and shaking hands—these are all customs about to be as dead as dinosaurs.

Little gender courtesies that I miss. Along with nongender courtesies between same-sex individuals such as "Thank you" and "May I help you with that?"

Little hallmarks of civilization.

It helps me to remember the little courtesies during discussions with friends about thorny subjects: the international situation, the economic situation, the religious situation, any situation.

It reminds me to mind my manners. To dredge up creaky habits of courtesy and civility. It keeps me from using phrases such as "ignorant and misguided." At least sometimes.

II

You know that annoying little song, "I'd like to teach the world to sing in perfect harmony?" So singsong cheerful that it was adopted as a commercial and became "I'd like to buy the world a Coke." Well, if I were to sing it, I would change the lyrics to "I'd like to teach the world to say thank you."

Have you noticed how out of favor this phrase has become? It's almost as archaic as "alas" or "verily." "Thank you" used to be a standard closure with salesclerks. Of course, that was before that awful ubiquitous phrase "Have a nice day" took over like jimsonweed.

But fewer and fewer clerks, especially young clerks, now say "thank you." I find the absence of this phrase unsettling, as if I am dangling in the air. So to fill the void, I find myself thanking them. Try as I might to break myself of the habit, I buy the merchandise, I pay for it, and as they hand it to me, I say automatically, "Thank you." For a while they replied automatically, "You're welcome." Now they're beginning to stop saying that. More and more I find that I can conduct entire sales transactions in silence. The reason salesclerks don't say "thank you," someone explained to me, is that they hate their jobs.

I was thinking about this when I met a couple of friends after work. They were crying in their beers about contemporary society and stress levels and being unhappy. One of them said, "I don't know a single person who's happy."

I said, "I am. I'm happy."

"You are?" one said. "Then you're the only person I know who is."

I did not stick around long. Nobody is more unpopular, I found out, than a cheerful soul amongst a bunch of sad sacks. Besides, what if unhappiness is contagious? I sure don't want to catch it.

Granted, a lot of being happy is good luck. Lucky to be healthy, lucky to have fulfilling work, lucky to be able to pay the bills. But I don't think all of it is luck. Abraham Lincoln said that he thought a fellow is about as happy as he makes up his mind to be.

At the same time I ran into my down-in-the-mouth friends, I was serving as foster mother to a pregnant cat from the animal shelter. Barely twenty-four hours after I settled her into my garage, she had a litter of kittens. I have become positively evangelical about the need for spaying and neutering dogs and cats. Most likely because of inadequate prenatal care and poor nutrition, the kittens had a bumpy start. One was born dead. Then mother and kittens got sick, the two smallest kittens died, and I nursed a third through serious illness; but eventually there they were—three fat and healthy kittens and a healthy mother cat.

Now, talk about happy. Nothing is happier than a tumble of kittens. Every day is a thrill to them. They bite one another's tail, they climb into my lap, supper dishes are filled, the sun comes up, and they're happy. They are roly-poly, furry personifications of the Zen philosophy described as the rapture of being alive.

It has been a great lesson for me. As the poet said, life is a crazy salad. And every day it is tossed anew: I bungle a project, I win an award, somebody I love is very ill, somebody I love has a wonderful vacation, three kittens die, three kittens live and frolic.

An enormously popular book by Sarah Ban Breathnach is *Simple Abundance,* about living life with joy, happiness, and contentment. One of the basic principles of this book is a sense of gratitude. Being thankful and grateful, the author says, has the power to transform our lives. Every night before we go to sleep, she says, we should write down in a gratitude journal five things we are thankful for that day. It is another way of saying, let's count our blessings. Or of saying, thank you.

Oh, wait.

Thank you for reading this.

September Is Be Kind to Editors and Writers Month

Book Tour

For years I have read about authors on their book tours. Oh, the exhaustion, they lament, promoting their new book from New York to Los Angeles. Oh, the weariness of limousines and wine receptions. Night after night in hotels, lines of people wanting autographed books, a murderous schedule of media interviews, and all the while weighed down by jet lag.

Let me tell you about my first Oklahoma book tour. It started in Eufaula, Oklahoma, where I spoke to the Friends of the Library, a lovely group of people who brought a covered dish lunch to hear my talk. From there, in fits and starts, I went elsewhere in Oklahoma: Broken Arrow, Kingfisher, Bristow, Tecumseh, Bartlesville, Norman, and more. Okmulgee is still thinking it over and has not officially ruled me out. I considered it a genuine tour if I drove on a highway to get there. I hit big cities, too, such as Tulsa and Oklahoma City.

Usually the audience was between thirty and a hundred people. Once it was an audience of five, and one of those was the author scheduled to speak after me. Another one was my publisher.

On one signing in a shopping mall, John Wooley—a fellow author—explained his philosophy of life: "The world is divided into two kinds of people," he said. "Those who buy my books and cheap bastards."

At one painful bookstore signing, my colleague Teresa Miller and I sat at our authors' table, our books stacked before us, our pens at the ready, smiling at people who came through the front door. The shoppers parted around us like the Red Sea. We looked at them with big puppy dog eyes, but it did no good. They averted their own eyes and busied themselves with their friends or their purses or their watches.

After about an hour with no customers, Teresa took out her cell phone and said, "I need to find a quiet place to make a call." She looked around the store and said, "Come to think of it, I guess this table is the quietest place here." Eventually a cousin of hers showed up and bought a book. Teresa's, not mine.

I signed books in bookstores and in shopping malls. I spoke to church groups, garden clubs, library associations, women's clubs, book clubs, and teachers. I spoke in libraries, schools, shops, restaurants, museums, churches, and private homes. It was not a circuit with a lot of author traffic; I did not run into Stephen King or Margaret Atwood. They don't know what they missed, because it was enormously rewarding to gather in small Oklahoma towns with people who love books, who build community, who educate children, and who raise families.

Everywhere I went, people listened to my stories and then told me theirs—caring for mothers with Alzheimer's, lives adrift after retirement, a teenage son who stormed out of the house during a family argument and was killed in a traffic accident, kindergarten teachers burned out by despair, college teachers sparkling with enthusiasm, happy newlyweds at age eighty, aspiring poets, widows with good recipes for breakfast casseroles, and elderly women well coifed and coping with degenerative retina disease. They told me their tales as cleanly and unemotionally as Hemingway prose. "The other morning I put frozen peas in my cereal instead of blueberries," a near-blind woman told me, and she laughed at this joke on herself. They told me how they had come to live in this state, about their life's work, their hobbies, and their families. These are the readers of Oklahoma. Our common language is books. The stories we read and the stories we live pull us together in a fabric of culture.

I spoke at Claremore, the home of Will Rogers, and I spoke at Nowata (population 3,800), my own hometown. I spoke in my hometown not once but four times. I began to identify with the writer S. N. Behrman, who said, "I've had just about all I can take of myself."

First, I was invited to the Nowata Historical Society, then to a teachers' meeting one Saturday morning at the First Christian Church, to a high school reunion, and finally to the historic Savoy Hotel for the one-hundredth anniversary of the garden club. My hosts were attentive to the details. At the historical society, my corsage matched the flowers on the tea table. The cookies and pastries and sandwiches and casseroles were homemade, and the volunteers had polished the silver service. The practical teachers had stacks of Styrofoam coffee cups. The garden club was polite to me but far more interested in the display of antique hats.

I have done lots of public speaking, but these talks in my hometown were hard gigs. They were the emotional pinnacles of my book tour. These audiences were former neighbors, teachers, schoolmates, and lifelong friends of my parents. They were people my mother and father had worked with, square danced with, gone fishing with. These were the people I wrote about—the ones in a small town who always knew who I was and what I was up to and called my mother and told her. I could not tell whoppers to this crowd, because they know all about me. I could not "address them"; that would be like delivering a lecture on the Mississippi transmigration experience at the breakfast table and expecting your family to raise their hands with questions.

I had to downshift, hard and fast, but I got to tell this hometown audience something I needed to hear me say. And that is how grateful I am to that little town for what it gave me—a strong work ethic, a solid education, a love of the arts and books. My little hometown did it with limited resources. A music teacher directed us in a school production of *Hansel and Gretel* and drove a carload of us to Tulsa to see professional opera singers in *Carmen* at the old municipal theatre. What great learning experiences those two musical events were for me. I was the Dew Fairy in *Hansel and Gretel,* and the day before the production, the music teacher told me I did not have to sing—I could just move my mouth—but the important thing was for me not to cut my long blond hair. At *Carmen,* I learned how hard it is to walk in French heels on a raked floor.

The teachers were there year after year, funny teachers like Mrs. Chouteau, who put the fear of algebra in us and who had a big pigeon bosom where she kept her hanky and her pocket money. Young Mrs. Clark taught us U.S. history with an intensity, a passion, and an intelligence we had never seen before. Mr. Moore helped us find part-time jobs and then met with us before school and during the lunch hour to teach distributive education. Do schools still have distributive education programs? I bought a used car and contact lens while earning sixty cents an hour.

I worked with the Kauffman Foundation in Kansas City, which funded a multimillion-dollar inner-city school (anti)dropout program. What I learned is that the scholarship money was important, but even more important to the students' success was the consistent presence of adults who cared about them. All of the students were from poor homes, many from broken homes, and some of them had no homes at all and slept in cars. What helped them succeed, the students told me, and what mattered most to them was the community of teachers, counselors, and staff that the foundation brought together to watch over them and to encourage them.

That is what we had in my hometown—a community that was an extension of family. At the time, I thought we had too damn much of it. I couldn't wait to leave my little hometown for a big city of blessed anonymity. I see it differently now. I value that sense of community. I am grateful to Mrs. Gillespie for loaning me books out of her front hall.

Who says you can't go home again?

October

Bring me the sunset in a cup

—Emily Dickinson, from poem 128

October Is Adopt-a-Dog Month

Bingo

I have the most implausible story to tell, and it all begins with a book I read titled *Clear Your Clutter with Feng Shui.*

The book says that clutter blocks energy and if we clear a space—or build a new space—new things will come into our lives to fill it. Am I ready for that.

So I built a new room on my house, a garden room, and sat down in it to see what new thing was going to come into it. Would it be a man, devastatingly handsome and moderately normal? A new job, with, dare I hope, easy work and high pay? An adventure? An exotic trip? I sat in my new room and tried to visualize all of these things—but it was hard to concentrate because of a dog's howling. Not howling so much as moaning, with a voice so sad that it was made of tears and despair.

I did not yet know it, but what had just come into my life was that dog. I, a committed, fanatical, almost pathological cat person, rescued a dog. What's more, he is a big dog, part German shepherd. And he is a sick dog that required medical treatment for everything under the sun including heartworms.

The person who had the dog tied it to the fence for three months, poured its dry food out on the ground without a dish, and did not scoop the small space but about once a week. Flies were eating the tips of the dog's ears raw. What's more, the human—not humane—was going to have the dog "put down"—a euphemism for killing. What's a soft-hearted cat person to do?

The dog and I looked at one another through the fence for a long moment. He was so sorrowful and sick, I gave him my word on the spot that everything was going to be okay. I would do everything I could to make it okay. We cannot change everything in this world, but this is one thing I could change. He came to live with me and a house-ful of appalled cats.

Still, it was a shock to everyone. Neighbors walked by at dusk chanting, "Connie Cronley has a do-og." And my calm, mature response was to shout, "Shut up, you big fat liar!" But I *did* have a dog.

The dog came with the name Bingo. My plan was to fence the back-yard and he would live there, with access to the garage. That plan lasted about a week; then he was in the house. My next plan was for him to stay in the new garden room, because I have all these cats. That plan lasted almost two weeks. By then Bingo had moved into the house and was sleeping beside the bed.

The cats hated his doggy guts. Bingo would walk through the house and I would hear explosions of hissing—Psss!—like tires exploding. One cat hissed so hard, she propelled herself backwards. All around the house, cats were arched with rigid fury, like so many croquet wickets. Bingo ignored them, which made them even more outraged. Slowly, the cats began tolerating him. All my human friends love him.

Bingo has one scarred ear that flops halfway down while the other ear points up. He is so happy to have a home, he walks around with a big, loopy grin on his face, looking like Walter Matthau. And he is smart. Within a week I had taught him to *sit* and to *go pee*. That is more than I have taught any other male in my life.

Our first walks with a leash through the neighborhood had neighbors doubled over with laughter as Bingo dragged me up and down the streets. Even a vagrant in the park laughed and called out, "Who is walking who?" For a while, we walked after dark.

When he was well enough, we enrolled in dog school. We attended the first session with some trepidation. Graduating from dog school is no sure thing. Jay, my ex-husband, was kicked out of dog school for two reasons; he would not do the homework and his dog bit an Afghan hound on the butt.

I may be only moderately trainable, but Bingo is quick and bright and he helps me along. He can now *sit, stay, come, walk,* and *heel* on a leash. He hates *down,* though. Refuses to do *down.* Maybe it's the word itself. Bingo has *been* down. Down on his luck, dragged down into depression, almost down and out. He has vowed never to be down again. What Bingo is going to be is happy, and grateful and grinning and most of all—*staying!*

October 14 Is Honey Bee Day

Southwestern Regionalisms

A stranger to these parts was mightily amused by a Southern expression of speech. It is the way we insert "God love him," into a criticism. We disavow the slur, the stranger said, as if we wanted to say it but did not want to own up to it.

Well, bless his heart, the stranger doesn't know what he's talking about. First of all, we are Southwesterners not Southerners. Big difference. To us.

Second, we do not disavow anything. Nothing. We can stand toe-to-toe and insult, slur, slight, criticize, and ridicule anybody, anytime. To your face or behind your back. Makes us no never minds.

The stranger, God love him, is as ignorant as a hole in the ground about us locals. The stranger, bless his heart, is as dumb as a dirt clod. As my daddy would say, he doesn't know "sic 'em from come here."

Here is the linguistic explanation. When we insert the phrase "bless his heart" or "God love her" into a criticism, what it means is that the poor, dumb fool can't help himself.

He can't help being as dull as a piece of string. It's not her fault she's as boring as watching paint dry. Bless their hearts, they're just afflicted with stupidity, sluggishness, and no sense of humor. Pathetic things. God's creatures, but pitiful.

Sometimes we use the adjective "poor" to stress their ignorant plight. In special cases, we emphasize the depth of our pity and irritation by salting the phrase with profanity: "Poor ignorant s.o.b."

However, we can also mean the terms genuinely—to express concern, to indicate empathy, to show affection and appreciation.

Another popular word we use in the South and Southwest is "honey." Any Southerner knows the multiple meanings of this word. I find that Yankees can be flummoxed by it. It can be used as a term of endearment or fondness, but it can often be used to sweeten a phrase or command: "Louie. Honey. Stop that."

It can be used to soften a threat: "Louie, honey, do you want to be put outside?"

It also can be used in sympathy. In this case, it is drawn out—"huh-nee"—and said almost musically. The following is a phone conversation I had with a tree removal firm that illustrates several uses of the word "honey" as a term of comfort.

One spring, a strong storm broke thousands of pounds of limbs off my great sycamore tree. The limbs fell on the house and across the front yard and blocked my driveway. I called Preuss Tree Service, but since the storm was widespread, it took several days for them to get to me.

A few weeks later, this being Tornado Alley, another storm came through and tore off more limbs of the same tree. This time I called the tree company before the sirens had stopped blowing. I spoke with Mrs. Preuss in a woebegone voice.

"Miz Preuss?" (Very soft and piteous.)

"Connie? Honey? Is that you?"

"Yes, ma'am."

"Did your tree fall on your house again, honey?"

"Yes."

"Well, honey! Bless your heart. I'll send the boys right over."
And she did. God love her!

Honey Recipes

I have read that ¼ cup of honey added to bathwater makes a luscious, scented bath that is good for the skin.

Hair Conditioner

½ cup honey
¼ cup olive oil (1 tablespoon for normal hair)

Mix together, work a small amount at a time through hair until coated. Cover hair with shower cap for thirty minutes. Shampoo well and rinse.

Courtesy of the National Honey Board.

Almond Honey Crunch

1 cup slivered almonds
¼ cup honey
1 tablespoon butter
1 tablespoon grated orange peel
Dash salt
2 ½ cups corn flakes

Combine almonds, honey, butter, orange peel, and salt in heavy frying pan. Cook over low heat, stirring constantly, until almonds are golden. Remove from heat. Add cornflakes and mix carefully. Spread on buttered baking sheet. When cool, break into small pieces.

Serves seven.

Courtesy of the National Honey Board.

The First Sunday in October
Is Intergenerational Day

Out of the Mouths of Babes

I met Ethan at church. It was love at first sight.

I can remember everything about him—his spiky hair, his blue shirt, his blue tie with a pink pattern, his leather suspenders, and his yellow Oshkosh socks.

He was carrying a shallow basket of offering to the altar when I first saw him. He lifted his foot high in a giant step to make the six-inch step and almost fell over backwards. Luckily his mom was beside him to help him regain his balance. His composure never wavered.

Ethan is three and a half.

Ethan and his mom came back to sit in the pew in front of me. After the service, I told him what a fine job he had done.

"Thank you, ma'am," he said, with just a little prompting from his mother. Then he turned and surveyed me and the three women sitting in the pew beside me. All of were us old enough to be his grandmother or even his great-grandmother. And with big, dark eyes twinkling he asked, "And who are you girls?"

We simpered and gushed and introduced ourselves. As the organ played the last chords, Ethan reminded us, "Don't forget—there are cookies downstairs."

Ethan and I are Episcopalians, and our church is gothic in architecture. We are very high church. We love incense and complicated music and stained glass and platoons of priests and deacons and oblationers in vestments the appropriate color for the church year. The Rite I service language is full of "thee," "thy," "beseech," and "vouchsafe." We bow and kneel and genuflect and cross ourselves until we are winded.

Clara was about four years old. I met her in church, too. She was skipping down the aisle holding her father's hand and wearing a party dress with lace stockings.

"What a lovely dress," I told her.

Unlike Ethan, Clara was not chatty. She was a lady of silence.

She answered me by holding up her treasure—half a communion wafer her father had given her.

"Look what you have," I exclaimed. "Lucky you."

Without a word, Clara broke it in two and gave half of what she had to me.

In our church, we have spent two thousand years polishing ceremony and prayer, and Ethan and Clara high stepped through it all, right to the heart of the matter. Sharing communion in church and cookies in the fellowship hall.

Amen.

October 16 Is Dictionary Day

Bob's Your Uncle

Interesting, isn't it, about the latest census report and the revelations of shifting demographics and ethnic populations? Now the SAT tests are falling out of grace: too white and upper middle class to be an accurate predictor of college performance. Everything changes, even change.

I was trying to read something that quoted correspondence from the fifteenth century and having a tough time because although it was in English, much of the vocabulary and spelling was foreign to me. It was as frustrating as trying to read something salted with Latin phrases or German words. You grasp the tail of the word, but then it wiggles away before you get your hands around it.

The struggle reminded me how much the English language changes—a kaleidoscope whirling into different shapes and colors. It also brought me face to face with one of my most unpleasant characteristics: I am a snob of the English language.

Being snobs means that we think we have more of something than other people do, and we are proud of it. More education or money or beauty. Being a snob of grammar or spelling is no less offensive than waving around a lot of clunky jewelry. Superior stances are precarious perches. I have to remind myself of that from time to time, and now is a good time to do it. In October, the garden is no longer a show-off and the trees are baring their souls. I can learn a lesson from that.

I went through a period of disdaining television as common, low-brow entertainment. Granted, this is accurate much of the time, but I balance that snooty attitude with an appreciation for popular culture. Our books and movies and music reflect our cultural identity, and I am happy to be part of it, sometimes applauding and sometimes sneering. That's my right. I go through phases of bemoaning the current slang for the way it cheapens our language, but then I remember that it is the verbal fad of the day, the linguistic equivalent of poodle skirts or grunge. That makes it fun and funny. Enjoy it, I tell myself, be entertained—because tomorrow, it's outta here.

I am especially amused by the phrases that indicate things that are passé and fleeting, such as "Oh, that is so ten minutes ago," or situations that are impossible or nonexistent, such as "That is definitely a not-happening thing."

Language is a tool as functional as a hammer when it communicates something clearly and directly, as elusive as a fragrance but no less communicative when it expresses something vague or expansive. A British friend of mine likes to end every toast by raising his glass and saying, "And Bob's your uncle." "What does that mean?" I've asked him. "Oh," he says with a wave of the hand, "a little of this and that and everything."

I discovered a wonderful euphemism in a biography of the stage actress Laurette Taylor. She was a stage star in the early 1900s and again at the end of her life in the works of a new playwright named Tennessee Williams. But in between, for twenty years, her life was a tragedy. She was alcoholic, sick, broke, unable to work. When her friends called to check on her, if Miss Taylor was too sick or too drunk to get out of bed, the maid answered the phone and told them euphemistically, "Madam is unavailable. She is motoring in the country."

I love that phrase. A genteel rendering of bleak despair.

Some days I feel like the cranky mayor in *The Music Man* who tells the young whippersnappers, "You watch your phraseology."

The phraseology that drives me to snarling is the ubiquitous reply "No problem." It has replaced the polite but archaic "You're welcome." Whenever someone does something for me—take out my groceries, lift my suitcase from the overhead bin, track down a product for me—and I offer them that old-fashioned boring "Thank you," they respond, "No problem."

Then, just as my hope for the future of communication was plummeting, I met three young people who have restored my faith in the spoken language. I was introduced to a chatty little girl with white-blond hair and eyes as blue as a prairie sky.

"My name is Maggie," she volunteered, "and I can spell it. Two g's. I'm five and a half, I go to preschool, I can read, and I LOVE cats." To make sure I understood, Maggie with two g's repeated this information for me several times, juggling the order for variety.

Matthew, who is four, pulled me aside at church to deliver a caution. "You don't want to be around cannons," he said. "They have fire and they make a loud noise."

Three-year-old Campbell came with his big sister, Hallie, who was trying to sell me merchandise to benefit her school. She held up the catalog and hawked cards and candy and wrapping paper, punctuating every sentence with the refrain "Don't touch anything, Campbell. Don't touch anything, Campbell."

Campbell did not touch anything. He stood statue still in the middle of the living room looking around while his sister extolled the virtues of chocolate and popcorn and tissue paper. Suddenly, Campbell joined the conversation with a show-stopping announcement. When his sister paused to take a breath, he blurted out, "I have new underwear."

Their vocabulary may be limited, their timing may be erratic, but Maggie, Matthew, and Campbell, none of them six years old, have mastered the art of communication. They understand clarity, succinctness, and enthusiasm, and they know what is important. They tell us the vital stuff, what we want to know about people: Who are you? Do you know yourself? What is important to you? What do you value? Can you avoid danger?

A time will come when friends and employers and romantic interests will go to great lengths to ferret out this information from Campbell, Matthew, and Maggie. In fifteen or twenty years, they will be saying the equivalent of "No problem" or "See you later, alligator." It will be okay, because they already have a bedrock self-knowledge of the big stuff: an interest in literature, kindness to animals, a passion for life, an appetite for learning, and good personal habits or, in simple words, new underwear.

It is time to shed my fussiness about the English language and read books from another culture. Perhaps I will buy myself some new underwear (lingerie, undergarments, foundation clothes, scanties) and read steamy Cuban novels. Maybe I will read more South American novels, Asian stories, and Mexican authors. I might watch some Australian and

New Zealand movies. Maybe I will dive into a stack of Walter Mosley mysteries and discover the black culture of Los Angeles in the 1940s and 1950s.

It is a great big world out there, and not all the people talk as I do. I want to know more about them. While I am alive and well and not motoring in the country, I want to be joyful and playful—and Bob's your uncle.

October 24 Is Black Cat Day

Two Cat Tales

I have a long-haired, black cat named Jesse James. He earned that name by hiding in the garage for three days after I adopted him. Jesse took a long time adjusting to life with me and the other cats. First he hid, then he went through a period of fighting. He is settled in now. When I lie on the sofa to doze through old movies, Jesse sleeps on my chest, his whiskers tickling my chin. It seemed to be a couple of years before I got a close look at him, but now I know that he has adorable white tufts between his toes.

On this holiday, however, I am talking about another cat I know all too well.

Oh what a frightening ordeal I have just been through with my cat, Sophie. She is a stub-tailed calico as round as a pie. She is a tough little kitty who spends a lot of time on the screened-in porch keeping a steely eye on the birds. Sometimes birds manage to get into the porch, and when that happens—lunchtime. Then I find telltale feathers in the house or, occasionally, a neat display of yellow beak and claws lined up beside Sophie's dish. The cat will be sprawled in a deep sleep somewhere—not a catnap but a heavy sleep. "Sophie darling," I say to her, "are you sleeping off a bird?"

I know I should be horrified at Mother Nature's red tooth, but it is hard to be morally outraged when I'm eating chicken.

As for Sophie, she is not horrified at all. She is a positive thinker. "Life is so good," Sophie thinks, "the birds wiggle through the screen to get to you."

But recently, Sophie has not been her perky self. For the past few months she has been lethargic, even for a cat. She sleeps all of the time and her appetite is off. At the sound of the can opener, the other cats thunder into the kitchen, but Sophie sleeps. When I am in my office, the other cats clamber over the desk. They are clever cats and know not to step on the keyboard, so they tiptoe through that tiny space between keyboard and computer—one after another, like so many high-wire performers. Sophie just sleeps.

Just before bedtime, at the manic cat period, the other cats race through the house, skidding around corners. Then they squabble over the best bed for the night. All but Sophie. She sleeps through it all.

So I took her to the veterinarian and said, "She's just not her usual self. She hardly eats more than a bite or two." Dr. Hammond poked and listened and looked and then said, "She looks okay, but she has lost a pound since she was here two months ago."

"Oh no," I cried. My fears were coming true. She *was* sick. So I called for blood tests. "Spare no expense," I said; "leave no stone unturned." I could hear the receptionist whistling merrily as she got out the adding machine. Tickety tickety—the expense mounted.

But the blood tests came back okay. Dr. Hammond found nothing wrong with her. "Sometimes it's like this," he said. "The cat looks fine, but it's a classic case of ADR."

"ADR—what's that?"

"Ain't doin' right."

I sniffled and snuffled all the way home. "Oh, Sophie," I said, "You've got ADR. A mystery ailment. A disease to baffle modern veterinary science." Tears streamed as I thought of her wasting away and my never knowing what's wrong with her.

I drove slowly home and I shuffled inside. My lamentations were as deep and dark as a coalmine. I was morose, forlorn, beyond consolation.

As for Sophie, she hopped out of the carrier and ate a hearty supper. Then she raced around the house. She has been eating heartily ever since. She is even back at her post on the screened porch, scanning the skies for succulent birdlings.

She was not sick at all. Who knows what it was? Maybe just a cat mood.

I don't know if I am an overly vigilant pet owner or just a scaredy-cat.

October 31 Is Halloween

Scary Parties

The first party I remember was a Halloween party my mother gave for my sister and me. I was about five years old. She improvised a gypsy costume for me. I had some kind of off-the-shoulder blouse, a full skirt, and huge, golden earrings made of the rings that go on canning jar lids. I wore lipstick. I was a blonde gypsy in dress-up play clothes, and I was devastatingly beautiful. I'm sure.

My parents loved giving parties for us kids. For one birthday party, my father hired a horse and wagon, and we went on a hayride out into the country to cook hot dogs. One of the boys did not show up on time, and Martha, his date, said, "Oh, go on and leave him. The jerk." The party was saved when we saw his parents' car hurrying to catch the wagon.

In the 1950s, my mother made children's party food that delighted us because it seemed marvellously grown-up: little sandwiches and real hors d'oeuvres of pickle, cheese, and wiener on a toothpick.

My parents rented the hall at St. Catherine's Catholic Church so I could host semiformal dances. All the kids pooled our collection of 45s. We had all taken dancing classes—the fox-trot and the waltz—but it was hell getting the boys to dance, although we girls looked glamorous in our semiformal dresses with lots of gathers at the bodice to give us shape. If it was a spring dance, the boys were more interested in putting June bugs on our bare necks or hanging around together outside. The chaperones had to keep shooing them back inside.

I go through party phases, giving teas, brunches, luncheons, cocktail parties. I am particularly fond these days of outdoor parties with vintage tablecloths and tables and chairs scattered on the lawn. I think I like that because it eliminates housecleaning and trying to keep the cat off the plate of egg salad sandwiches covered with a damp dish-towel. I have grown so lazy, I have almost stopped giving dinner parties, but recently I was driven into it by fear.

I had developed a temporary anxiety—I was afraid that nobody will come to my funeral. I was tormented by memories of funerals so big that the church couldn't hold all the mourners, delays while extra seats were set up in the aisle, while sound systems were rigged to accommodate the crowd outside. That is what I want, not a handful of people trying to remember who I was and rattling around an empty church like beads in a drawer.

I became so distracted by this worry, instead of giving the cat her pill I swallowed it myself; now I have something else to fret about.

This concern about posthumous neglect propelled me to the scary experience of hosting a dinner party. At first, I was excited about it. I worked arduously to get the guests assembled on a given date. This was the perfect gathering—bright, artistic, witty people. I planned the menu carefully. I decided on the table setting and the flowers. This is going to be so wonderful, I thought. This evening is going to sparkle.

And then, when the week of the dinner party came, I changed my mind. I could never measure up to the stylish dinner parties given by my chums. Anna and Joe have entertainment between the main course and dessert. Jane and Jim host book club dinners centered around books that mention food—and prepare the food from the books. Melissa and Mike's Thanksgiving dinners are so long and elaborate that they feature a Turkey Trot, which is a brisk walk around the block after cocktails and before we sit down at the table.

Mostly, though, it was not fear of competition that led me to change my mind. It was sloth. I didn't want to clean and cook and entertain. I wanted to lie down and read a book. There was the shopping and the traffic was nightmarish. I had to go four places to get the food. And everywhere I went, I saw that what I had just bought was cheaper at this place.

Then there were the alerts that had to be posted among the guests before they arrived. Subjects that could not be discussed. We could not talk about books, because one was a writer and had just had a nasty experience with a publisher. Music was out, either as a subject or as background entertainment, because one was a musician having some kind of professional crisis. Pets were off-limits because one had a sick cat and wept every time an animal was mentioned. The subject of children is always delicate, best to be avoided because of the various misadventures of assorted progeny. Politics and economics were far too incendiary for our fragile psyches.

I was at a posh dinner recently where the unacquainted guests were thrown together by a meeting. They were so wary of blundering into explosive conversational territory, the only safe ground they could find to discuss was what years they had graduated from college. Once that was exhausted, and a long silence endured, they began surveying one another to discover what years they had graduated from high school.

For my own party, I thought about posting at the door a list of delicate subjects to be avoided and letting my guests add to it as they came in.

By the time the dinner hour arrived, I was so cranky that all I wanted to do was sit in the kitchen by myself. I thought that I would go into the dining room now and then to slap down plates in front of them, then go back into the kitchen to drink coffee.

No, that wouldn't work, I decided, because there was no door to the kitchen. They would merely trail in after me demanding coffee for themselves. And since there was not time to get a door put on the kitchen, I had to see it through.

The guests arrived with their arms full of flowers and wine and treats for my naughty cats. Suddenly, during dinner, my calico cat, Sophie, leapt in an arching *grand jeté* to the center of the table and walked down the length of it, delicately stepping around candles and serving dishes to visit her favorite human. The guests were in such good spirits that they thought it was charming.

We started the meal with bruschetta made with the last of the garden's fresh tomatoes and basil and spread on toasted peasant bread; we ended it with freshly baked pound cake. And through it all, the guests laughed and talked and told funny stories until the whole evening glowed like candlelight.

What a wonderful idea, I thought as I was cleaning up, an autumn's supper party to start the season feeling bountiful in friends and food.

On a trip to Paris, I took a cooking class at the Ritz Escoffier (École de Gastronomie Française), and this is a dish the chef taught us to make. I have simplified the directions and modified the ingredients, but I left in enough of the original to give you the Ritz flavor. This is one of my favorite appetizers to serve at dinner parties.

Crepes of Salmon and Guérande Sea Salt

4 thin slices of raw salmon (I use lox.)
7 ounces fresh goat cheese
olive oil (amount is vague)
1 ¾ ounces black olives (I omit these.)
6 teaspoons heavy cream
1 teaspoon salt from Guérande (I don't know what this is.)
1 teaspoon black pepper
1 bunch chervil and 1 bunch dill (I use chives or basil or
    tarragon from my herb garden instead. Chives are going to
    be needed later anyway.)
Juice of two lemons

Season the salmon slices with salt and pepper (I don't do this) and brush with lemon juice for a shine.

Chop herbs finely.

Mix goat cheese, olive oil, herbs (the French recipe did not mention chives in the ingredients but calls for it here), and cream.

Use a piping bag with plain nozzle to pipe out a small quenelle (dumpling) of the cheese mixture on each slice of salmon. (I do it without the piping bag. I'm not French.)

Roll and wrap tightly in plastic wrap and refrigerate for at least one hour.

Make a vinaigrette dressing by using the remaining lemon juice and olive oil along with the dill and chervil (detached from stems).

To serve: Put a parcel of salmon on the bottom of each plate, add the mixed herbs along with the roughly chopped black olives, and finish by sprinkling the salt from Guérande and the pepper over the salmon. Add a dash of olive oil. (I don't do this, either.)

I slice the rolls into pieces and serve as hors d'oeuvres.

November

The Frost himself so comely
Dishevels every prime
Asserting from his Prism
That none can punish him

—Emily Dickinson, from poem 1236

November 8 Is Cook Something Bold and Pungent Day

Holiday Cheer

What I thought we would do today, as a public service for holiday entertaining, is review some of the guidelines for being a good hostess. This is inspired by god-awful parties I have hosted and nightmarish functions I have attended.

Let's begin with the toughest—TV football parties. Televised games of collegiate competition can transform a pleasant party into a brawl before you can grab the crystal dish of dip off the coffee table. One football party that I attended ended with guests, giddy with victory, merrily throwing furniture onto the roof. Another football party took a darker turn at kickoff. A guest laughed at the home team, and the co-host—who happened to be my husband—stormed out of the house, leaving the startled guests blinking, me smiling brightly, a piping-hot casserole, and some three hours left in the game. So, Advice No. 1—be wary of mixing parties and football games over the holidays unless you are young and resilient.

Advice No. 2—Hospitality. This is also tricky, especially if alcohol is involved. At one holiday party, I chattered politely at the hostess as she stared bug-eyed at something behind me. I turned around to see her husband passionately kissing a guest I had brought. We want our guests to feel welcome in our homes, but not that welcome. It may not seem fair, but even during the holidays, there is no moratorium on those pesky commandments about coveting and adultery.

At the other extreme, I have known hosts who take the occasion of the dinner party to soliloquize on subjects of interest only to them. On and on they drone, monologue after monologue, while guests suffer blank faced. Let us remember that the root word of "hospitality" is akin to "hospital" and "hospice" and refers to sheltering and entertaining guests, not boring them into a coma.

I pulled a list of entertainment tips off the Web titled "The ABC's of Entertaining," which begins this way: *A* is for attitude—are you into formal or casual entertainment? *B* is for budget. *C* is for corporate entertaining . . .

That's where it lost me. No, no. *C* is for cats at a party.

A futile debate is whether or not it is acceptable for cats to be on the table. Or kitchen counter. Or furniture. When guests are present. My position is that it is the responsibility of the guests to know in advance if the hostess has a cat or cats (plural) and, if so, to assume that said cats will be wherever they choose to be. Discipline does not apply. Think of the Rhett Butler line, "Frankly, my dear, I don't give a damn." Any cat could have said that.

So, Advice No. 3 is about pets. Remember that the pets live there; if you are a guest, you don't. A hostess gift for the pet would be a nice touch.

Advice No. 4 has to do with ambiance and decoration. It could be the people I know, but in my experience, one must be very careful about mixing guests and candles. At one awful dinner party, a guest red-faced with emotion leaned over the table to shout at someone, and the candles set his tie on fire. This gave the other guest occasion to throw a glass of water on him. Episodes like this can almost ruin dessert.

And that brings us to Advice No. 5, which is about food. We all know how important food is to a function. One of my favorite books is titled *Murder on the Menu,* with recipes suitable for events in murder mysteries such as "What to Serve until the Coroner Comes" or "A Light Repast before the Inquest."

My friend Deanna gave me a charming little antique book of menus and recipes titled *Suppers and Midnight Snacks.* It includes chapter titles such as "A Frivolous Spring Supper for Six," "A Plebeian Soufflé for Four," and "A Winter Supper for Eight Serious Eaters."

I am delighted that Deanna thinks of me as a hostess who will make special food for lawn parties, beach suppers, and midnight meals.

However, this is tempered by the bitter memory of an invitation to a potluck party of a few excellent women. The list of homemade dishes to be brought was slung around with heady abandon—a cream cheese appetizer topped with caviar, a ham loaf accompanied by spicy horse-radish sauce, potatoes with onions and fresh dill, poached fruits in wine. "What about me?" I asked. "What do you want me to bring?" The hostess studied me for a moment, reading the very soul of my culinary abilities. Then she said, "Do you think you could bring—a jar of pickles?"

Perhaps I will not entertain at all this holiday season. Perhaps I will cook something simple for myself—an onion tart, maybe, or a hearty stew—and read about cooking. I will reread something by the all-time finest food writer, M. F. K. Fisher: perhaps her memoir *As They Were* or *The Gastronomical Me,* two of the most sensual books ever written about people, places, and food.

Once Ms. Fisher was asked why she devoted her career to writing about food, and she said that when she writes about food, she is writing about our three basic needs—food, security, and love. They are so mixed and mingled, she said, that we cannot think straightly about one without the others. She said, "When I write about eating bread on a hillside or drinking red wine in a room, I remember the situation, the people who went with it, and the deeper needs for love and happiness. So writing about food in the bowl is also writing about nourishment in the heart."

Bon appetit and happy holidays.

November 8 Is National Ample Time Day*

I Need to Tell You

The e-mail began, "I need to tell you . . ."

The e-mail came from the *Jolly Moon,* Dan and Molly's boat, harbored in Jamaica. They retired early a couple of years ago and have been sailing ever since. Recently they were working at a school in Jamaica and raising money for a children's pan band, whatever that is.

The e-mail came on a Saturday morning in June, a day rare for its sweetness. In Oklahoma, summer is starting to heat up in June. It is either too dry or too wet. Humidity is high, thanks to the state's having more miles of lakeshore than any other state in the continental United States, and it is often so windy that you cannot eat outside or your sandwich will blow into Osage County. This, however, was a particularly lovely June day, suitable for brides or picnics or gardening. Or for dozing in a lawn chair thinking of combining those elements: gardening brides on a picnic. Picnicking brides in a garden.

The e-mail came when I was at a coffee shop drinking latte with my friend Diane. The frenetic school term/winter work schedule had ended, and summer stretched ahead of us. We drank latte, ate blueberry muffin tops, and caught up with our lives. Her son had visited colleges and chosen one. Her teaching schedule and her course work for a doctorate were slowed until fall. Our mutual friends were leaving for the summer, going to their second homes in Montana and Nova Scotia. We, left behind for an Oklahoma summer, smiled tightly and hoped they had a nice time.

"How about you?" Diane asked. "How was your book talk last week?"

I had spoken to a garden club and then signed books in my hometown.

* National Ample Time Day is a day to make time for the priorities in life and to live a completely fulfilling life.

"Great," I said. "Fun. Stressful. I came home, went to bed at five-thirty and slept for eighteen hours." Hometowns are one thing. Small, rural hometowns are a whole different enchilada.

The downtown traffic light is now just a stop sign. The upscale department store is now a gift store. The hamburger drive-in where my high school friends and I devoted countless hours to trying to persuade the carhop that we really were eighteen and could buy beer is now a funeral home. The Ponyboy, the fun bar where genuine eighteen-year-olds went and where the rest of us drove behind (so that our parents would not know we were there trying to get our older friends to buy beer for us) is now an H&R Block. Wal-Mart, which drove many small businesses out of business, left town and was replaced by a dollar store.

Main Street is missing so many buildings, it looks like a jack-o-lantern.

My family home, my grandmother's house, my aunts and uncles' houses—all sold to strangers.

Many of the ladies from the garden club had been neighbors, teachers, friends of my parents. They came with bouquets of memories of my family.

Visiting my rural, small hometown broke my heart. It seemed like a dead rose, a dry version of the vibrant town I knew. In fragments and flashes I remember the life that was there. The scandals, the vendettas, the mischief, the love affairs, the work, the boredom, the action. It was not the town that was sad, it was that while I wasn't looking, pieces of my life had faded and blown away on the prairie wind.

Change is inevitable, change is good, change is life. Change hurts. I heard an interview on public radio with an artist who photographs flowers in all stages, from buds to crumbling dead blossoms. What her photographs show, she said, is that every stage of the life cycle is beautiful.

And that is how it was speaking to the garden club in my hometown. It is easier not to see the changes.

And yet. When my father died, I sat alone all one night on the balcony feeling grief like a living thing in my chest. As painful as this is, I thought, I don't ever want this wound to close completely. I want to keep a sliver of it tender, open, and in touch with feeling. That is the part of me that feels life. That is the part of me that connects me to the rest of the world.

Meanwhile, Cinnamon is pregnant. So is Gina. Michele's birthday is tomorrow. Are we renewing our Concertime season tickets? Your hair looks great that way. I have been trying for three months to lose ten pounds. It's been too wet for my petunias, but my hollyhocks, which also like hot, dry weather, are blooming for the first time, so what is that about? Did you see the story in this morning's paper about "fluffing" your house? It's a new term for rearranging the furniture and rotating your stuff on display. Is that not a great idea? I'm going home to fluff my living room and see if that doesn't revitalize me.

"What we need to do," Diane said, "is fluff our *lives*."

"Great idea!" I said. "I am in such a rut just working every day. I'm not having any fun, just the same routine. I can't get up in the morning knowing how much work is crouching outside the door waiting for me. And no matter how much I work, I can't catch up."

Okay, we agreed, as soon as she gets back from (wherever) and as soon I am through with (whatever), we are going to fluff our lives. We are going to play some. We are going to plan a day trip. To the Tall Grass Prairie, maybe. Or maybe a trip of a couple of days to go to Archer City, Texas, to visit Larry McMurtry's famous bookstores. Or there's always Kansas City or Dallas.

As soon as. Solemn pledge. Starting this summer.

Back home, before I started my house fluffing, I checked my e-mail.

The e-mail came from the *Jolly Moon,* harbored in Jamaica.

"I need to tell you," Molly wrote, "Dan died last night."

Thanksgiving Is the Fourth Thursday of November

Dump Thanksgiving

Well, eat up, because my guess is, Thanksgiving is on its way out. I think it is only a matter of time before we see the last of Thanksgiving as a major holiday. I don't mean a Dump Thanksgiving campaign. I mean something more subtle–just ignore it until it is forgotten.

I base this on the fact of how fast the stores yank Halloween merchandise off the shelves and replace it with Christmas things. As the marketers might say, nothing personal, but Thanksgiving just doesn't deliver. With Thanksgiving you've got no gifts, no flowers, no costumes, because who wants to go as a Pilgrim? A few greeting cards maybe, but except for the turkey and cranberry industries, zip.

Thanksgiving is all about family and food and that, frankly, is not sexy enough. It doesn't sell. For sexy we've got Valentine's Day—lingerie, perfume, flowers, cards, candy and cakes in erotic shapes, romantic weekend retreats, naughty dancers delivering singing messages. With Valentine's Day, we've got real marketing opportunity. Take imagination and add commercialism and you've got a bang-up, high-dollar holiday.

But Thanksgiving? About as dull as President's Day, which is so unmarketable that Washington and Lincoln now have to share a day. Thanksgiving is just a tick away from the other unsexy holidays: Labor Day, Memorial Day, and Martin Luther King Day. Not even among the moderate sellers such as Mother's Day or St. Patrick's Day. Not an up-and-coming sales holiday like Boss's Day or Secretary's Day and perilously close to deadbeat holidays such as May Day, Flag Day, and United Nations Day. Hardly anything to buy then.

Used to be, a holiday was a time to commemorate, remember, observe something, maybe have the day off, and rest or play. Now the attitude seems to be, if a holiday can't sell something, what good is it?

Besides, it will not be as if November is left without days to celebrate food. In case you did not know it, November is Peanut Butter Lovers' Month. One whole week is dedicated to celebrating split pea soup, and there is a day in November set aside for Sandwich Day, sponsored appropriately enough by Ziploc Sandwich Bags. And for those of us who didn't know it before now, November 24 is Sinkie Day, promoted by the International Association of People Who Dine over the Kitchen Sink. The Sinkie world headquarters is in Santa Rosa, California.

So there will be plenty of opportunities remaining in November to honor food.

And if we worry that without Thanksgiving there won't be a day to celebrate family, what about November 18, Mickey Mouse's birthday? Surely that counts—Minnie and Goofy and Pluto. That's a family.

So let the commercial world rule. Dump Thanksgiving. Go directly from Halloween to Christmas, then through New Year's with all the hype of party clothes and champagne to January 8, which is The King's birthday. Now there's a holiday with marketing potential. We haven't begun to peak on selling Elvis memorabilia.

And someday, some dreamy old-timer can ask, "Didn't there used to be another holiday in November? Seems like it was such a big deal when I was growing up. You know, the one with all the pies."

And someone will answer, "I think I remember that. Wasn't it Sadie Hawkins Day?"

November Begins the Peak Sales for Celery

Celery, the Faded Darling of the Dinner Table

Oh, it is a two-edged sword, the sharp sunlight of winter. The outdoors is brilliance edged with dramatic shadows. Inside, the ruthless sunshine highlights every grimy light switch, dusty ceiling fan, and dirty carpet.

I looked around the house with a dismay that almost made me swoon. Then I rallied. I turned to Phoebe the cat and declared, "Never let it be said that I abandoned my art for vacuuming."

Mercifully, the winter days are short. Happily, the nights are long. Perfect for a lazy woman. I climb onto the sofa, pile cats high around me, and watch marathons of old movies.

And that is how I discovered celery.

First, in *Meet Me in St. Louis,* a movie set in 1903, I saw Judy Garland's upper-class Edwardian family eating celery at the dinner table. The celery stalks seemed to be a featured item of their meal. Then, in *The Bishop's Wife,* a 1947 movie, another dinner table featured celery. Cary Grant said to David Niven, "Please pass the celery." Not great dialogue but informative to me.

I may not have a burning energy for housecleaning, but suddenly I was possessed with a curiosity about celery.

I like cream of celery soup, enjoy celery sticks, and nibble on celery stuffed with cheese, but I have never considered these to be great delicacies. It is just—celery. The celery shown in the movies, however, was not matchstick hors d'oeuvres but rather whole stalks of celery. David Niven passed a low plate of it.

"What the . . . ?" I asked myself. What I learned from dabbling in research on the computer is that celery may have been brought to the New World in the 1600s, but it was not popularized or commercially grown in this country until the late 1800s. A Scots farmer in Kalamazoo cultivated a modern variety in 1856. Dutch farmers in the area began producing it as a cash crop. The cold-weather plant, with its shallow root system, flourished in Michigan's swampy muck lands. By 1890, vendors were selling the new vegetable to passengers on trains passing through the area. Kalamazoo billed itself as Celery City.

Suddenly, celery was the chichi thing on society tables. The vegetable was rare and pricey, so it was served in silver or fine cut-glass. I knew a woman who collected pressed-glass celery vases. These are similar to pressed-glass spooners (squat vases designed to hold spoons). Just as spoons once symbolized wealth and hospitality, special vases were created to showcase them. Celery vases are slightly taller and footed and often have a scalloped top. These were quite popular in the 1880s, when celery stood proudly, almost the centerpiece of the Victorian table. An article in the *Ladies' Home Journal* in 1891 explained how to serve celery. It was to be put on the table with the meat course along with other vegetables and removed before dessert.

Gradually, but through no fault of its own, celery's status fell. New varieties of the vegetable were easier to produce, so it was no longer rare. As celery fell in grace, so did its serving pieces. Celery began to be served in low serving dishes, as used in the Cary Grant–David Niven movie.

The stately cut-glass celery vases are now collector's items. Antiques guides warn us not to confuse celery vases (usually six to nine inches tall) with spooners (four to six inches tall). Both may be stemmed and have scalloped edges, but spooners are narrower. Then, too, there is the danger of demonstrating coarse ignorance and buying an open sugar bowl, goblet, or tumbler thinking it is a celery vase. Or a spooner.

Celery is a native plant of the Middle East and Mediterranean. The Greeks, Romans, and Chinese ascribed medicinal, decorative, and flavoring properties to it. As a wild plant, it is known as smallage, which does not grow in North America. It's a cousin of carrots, parsley, and parsnips, all of which are members of the Umbelliferae family. The plant that we most often buy today is the variety Pascal, the celery first grown on Dutch celery farms in Michigan.

In the late 1890s, a celery tonic was available in the Sears Roebuck and Company catalog. My *Fanny Farmer Cookbook* lists oodles of recipes for celery—as an appetizer (stuffed with caviar or seasoned cream cheese), folded into cranberry jelly, as a salad garnish (celery hearts cut into "curls" or served "club style"), made into relish, sauce, soup, and cooked as a vegetable.

Granted, my cookbook is the eleventh edition, published in 1965, but the preface assures me that the book remains true to the first edition, published in 1896. I like to think of turn-of-the-century cooks preparing and serving celery as a vegetable. Celery pieces one to three inches long were boiled or braised for fifteen to twenty minutes in salt water, consommé, or stock, then topped with butter or a cream sauce.

Celery consumption peaked in the United States in 1946, when postwar diners ate 9.1 pounds per capita. The next year, by the time *The Bishop's Wife* came out, the crunchy vegetable had plummeted to 7.9 per capita. It has averaged about 7 pounds per person ever since.

Now the United States produces two million pounds of celery a year, mostly in California (two-thirds), followed by Florida (one-fifth) and Michigan. Justifiably proud of its celery history, Portage, Michigan, has a celery museum.

Since marketers analyze things with a vengeance, demographic studies reveal that men eat more celery than women do, that people aged sixty and over eat more celery than any other age group does, and that blacks eat less celery than whites do.

Celery is rich in vitamin C and potassium and is low in calories. Two stalks have about twenty calories, but it is a myth that we burn more calories than that chewing it.

These days, none of us eat much Waldorf salad, crisp with apples and celery, but we use celery in chow mein, stews, and gumbo. Since celery is used in most stuffing recipes, sales reach their zenith in November and December.

Ogden Nash wrote a verse about celery:

> Celery raw
> develops the jaw.
> But celery, stewed,
> is more quietly chewed.

Advent Begins the Sunday
Nearest November 30

Advent

You know how, if nobody is looking, you pick through a bowl of mixed nuts to get the best ones? I hate to confess it, but that is how I am about my religion.

One of my favorite times to be Episcopalian is Advent. Not many denominations recognize Advent, and I don't know how many denominations are serious about Advent besides us, the Lutherans, and the Roman Catholics—and some of *us* aren't too serious about it.

Lest you get the idea that Episcopalians are solemn people preoccupied by prayers, we are fond of Episcopalian jokes, such as, You Know You Are an Episcopalian if . . .

- When you hear the phrase "May the force be with you" from *Star Wars,* you automatically answer, "And also with you";
- There is often wine at a church meeting;
- You automatically genuflect or bow as you enter a row of seats in a theatre.

Advent means "the coming," anticipating the arrival of Christ. The liturgical colors are royal blue or purple. It is a season of Advent wreaths and calendars. Advent begins near St. Andrews Day and lasts for four weeks.

It is a season for waiting, looking inward, and quietly, starkly anticipating the joy of Christmas. Traditionally, we Episcopalians do not put up a Christmas tree until Christmas Eve, do not sing carols until Christmas Day, and then celebrate for twelve days until Epiphany.

I don't know any Episcopalian who does this except me, and, just between us, it is because Advent happens to fit my current reclusive attitude, which is under-the-bed for the holidays. I have been driven to this by the pervasive popular, secular holiday music: yet another soulful version of "Little Drummer Boy" and still another jaunty "Jingle Bell Rock."

By the end of December, I hate any bell that jingles. I hate Alvin and the Chipmunks and the snowman in the meadow named Parson Brown. I hate all of those brave, pitiful holiday characters—the Little Match Girl, the Littlest Angel, and Tiny Tim. I hate that crybaby Clara with her broken Nutcracker.

It's hard to stay happily quiet during the holidays. Hard to resist parties with people I don't care to spend time with, hard not to buy stuff for people whose homes already look like a curiosity shop. Some Decembers I welcome the annual cold or sinus infection that keeps me inside because once I'm out there—once I'm on the streets, in the stores— hang on, here I go. I am going through Utica Square at a dogtrot, grabbing bottles of exotic olive oil, expensive bath oils, quaint cookie cutter packages, richly scented candles. You name it and I have just bought it for, oh, I don't know, somebody will turn up.

No sir, give me Advent.

November Is Peanut Butter Lovers' Month

Just Gimme a Sandwich and a Glass of Milk

When the calendar rolled over to 2000, when some were running for cover crying, "Y2K's gonna get you if you don't watch out," the *New York Times* took a higher road and published several magazines of highlights of the millennium. One magazine, which I have seen only on the Internet, was about women. I have a special interest in this subject because I have been a woman for, oh gosh, what seems like a thousand years.

Through the magic of computers, here was a chance to ask questions about etiquette and get the answers from three experts through the years.

The question I chose was a question that certainly haunts me: How should a table be set when no company is expected?

In 1861, the expert Isabella Beeton would have told me that a mistress should rise by seven o'clock at the latest and be ready to descend to the breakfast room at eight with key-basket in hand. There I should ring at once for the tea, coffee, cocoa, or chocolate, according to the season, and let my eye glance over the table to see that everything is in its place and ready for the family—flowers on the table, preserves or marmalade in cut-glass dishes.

In 1923 Emily Post would say that whether there is company or family alone, the linen must be spotless and the silver clean. Company manners and everyday manners must be identical in service and in family behavior. And, Emily Post said, there is no excuse for wilted flowers or an empty vase.

And in 1999, Amy Vanderbilt said the difference is that a formal table requires classic flatware, china, and crystal, while the informal setting allows bolder colors and more freedom. For example, napkins need not match tablecloths.

Then I read about historic cookbooks.

When I was first married, the cookbook I bought was Fanny Farmer's. I like her recipe for chicken cacciatore. I still make tomato aspic from her recipe. I don't know anybody else who makes tomato aspic at all.

Fanny Farmer's book was published originally in 1896 as the *Boston Cooking School Cook Book* and has evolved through thirteen editions and has sold more than three million copies.

Fanny Farmer was a red-haired, brisk, energetic, opinionated woman who had a hearty appetite. She was ahead of her time in understanding the importance of good nutrition. She was a passionate cook and a teacher who told her readers how to judge the freshness of fish, how to select good poultry and game, what cuts of meat to buy, what was important to a well-balanced diet, and to buy fresh eggs. She believed that good bread is our most important food.

Her greatest impact on American cooking was the admonishment to measure ingredients, and so she became known as "the mother of the level measurement."

One hundred years ago, a dinner party was a robust affair for both cook and diner. Here is a menu from Fanny Farmer's original 1896 cookbook, all twelve courses.

The first course begins with either clams or oysters and brown-bread sandwiches.

The second course is soup (often two soups—one clear, one cream). Radishes, celery, or olives are passed after the soup.

The third course is bouchées or rissoles with a filling of light meat.

The fourth course is fish with coleslaw.

The fifth course is roast saddle of venison or mutton, spring lamb, or fillet of beef with potatoes and one other vegetable.

The sixth course is an entrée made of light meat or fish.

The seventh, eighth, and ninth courses are vegetables, cheese, and game with a vegetable salad.

The tenth course is cold dessert.

The eleventh course is frozen dessert and fancy cakes. Bonbons are passed after this course.

And the twelfth and final course is cheese, crackers, and café noir served in the drawing and smoking rooms. Brandy for the men and sweet liqueur for the women, or crème de menthe for all, may be served after the café noir. And of course there are guidelines for what wines and liquors are to be served with the other courses.

After all of that, I am amazed that women made it through the past thousand years. And I am proud to be the descendant of these key-basketed, flower-arranging, well-mannered, cooking amazons.

But once in a while, just gimme a peanut butter sandwich and a glass of milk.

December

Some keep the Sabbath going to Church—
I keep it, staying at Home—
With a Bobolink for a Chorister—
And an Orchard, for a Dome—

—Emily Dickinson, from poem 324

Christmas Pageants—December Is Read a New Book Month

Classics

The two books I wish I had written are *To Kill a Mockingbird* and *The Best Christmas Pageant Ever.*

Both are classics, both tell big messages from a child's perspective, and both are funny.

The Best Christmas Pageant Ever features the Herdmans—six children described this way in the book: "The Herdmans were absolutely the worst kids in the history of the world. They lied and stole and smoked cigars (even the girls). They talked dirty, hit little kids, cussed their teachers, and set fire to Fred Shoemaker's old broken-down toolhouse."

Who would have thought that a story about the worst kids in the history of the world would become a Christmas classic? In the slender book, the Herdmans finagle their way into taking over the church Christmas pageant. Imogene Herdman bullies her way into being Mary and says, "Who named the baby Jesus? I would have named him Bill." When the chaos ends—and the fire truck has driven away—all of us have a new look at the meaning of Christmas.

In 1972, Barbara Robinson created the six Herdman kids for a magazine Christmas story. The story generated so much reader mail, she expanded it into the eighty-page book. Students, librarians, parents, and ministers fell in love with the rascally Herdmans.

Publishers Weekly described it as one of the best Christmas books ever. The book became so popular, Robinson adapted it into a play and then into a successful movie. Thirty years later, the book is considered a classic and has sold more than two million copies worldwide. It is classified as a children's book, but I did not discover it until I was an adult. I laugh aloud every time I reread it, and I give copies as gifts to my adult friends. I am such a fan of the book, I arranged to interview the author for a newspaper story.

Miss Robinson spoke to me from her home in Berwyn, Pennsylvania, about writing the classic. "I had no idea it would do this," she said. Neither did she consider it a children's book. She was a short story writer and wrote it as a family story. When she was commissioned to write a Christmas article for *McCall's Magazine,* she flipped through a children's picture book for inspiration and was struck by the nativity's familiar language, "It came to pass . . ."

She wondered about kids who had never heard the nativity story or biblical-language story. "I realized they would be fairly wild and woolly," she said. That was the beginning of the incorrigible Herdmans— six skinny kids who live over a garage, who grow poison ivy instead of grass in the yard, and who "emptied the whole first grade in three minutes flat" at show-and-tell.

Part of the book's popularity is because it is a holiday book, she said. "And I suspect because of its multigenerational appeal. It does seem to last through the years."

Her books are not for very young children, Robinson says, and she advises her readers not to do what the Herdmans do, either in the Christmas book or the sequel *The Best School Year Ever.* When I spoke with her, she was writing a book about the Herdmans at Halloween, which is a scary thought. That third book about the Herdmans, she said, "was supposed to be finished two years ago, but writing funny books is slow work. I wish I were a faster writer. I wish I were more prolific. I'm not. Humor is so fleeting. You have to catch it on the run."

The Halloween Herdmans book has been published, and now, she said, "I'm going to send them to summer camp."

Miss Robinson travels extensively, visiting schools to talk about reading and writing. Students always ask her if the Herdmans are real or make-believe. "I never knew a whole family of them," she answers, "but like any other kid in school, there were people I avoided."

She reports encouraging news from her visits with schoolchildren across the country. "Television or not," she said, "kids are reading. They're reading more than we think they are. And they are writing."

School visits are dependent on discretionary funds, she said, and her guest appearances slow down when the economy flags. "The schools really try. I'm so impressed with the efforts librarians and teachers put forth to bring artists, writers, and musicians into schools. I asked a teacher, 'Does this pay off for you? It's very expensive for you—not just money, but teachers' time and preparation.' And she said, 'It's gravy for the students at the top of the spectrum. They're going to read and write anyway. For them, it's extra. The children at the bottom, maybe two or three will benefit. But all the kids in the middle get raised a notch.'"

Her own taste in clothes is black, beige, and oyster, "but when I go to schools," she told me, "I wear red, because children respond to that. They like the color."

Her advice to aspiring writers is "First, to read. Because it forms your taste without your knowing it. The number one thing everyone says is 'Write every day.' Find a time. I tell them, 'Your lives are very busy, but find a time—even if it's only fifteen to twenty minutes. Write something. If you're not involved in a story at the time, look out the window and write what you see. Invent a family across the street and put them into a story. Write something every day and then it becomes a habit."

When people ask her about her own writing schedule, she told me, "I lie a little bit. I tell people what everybody says, that you've got to have a set time. It's a fact that when I'm home and not traveling, I try to go to my workplace about nine in the morning and stay there without doing anything else until about two in the afternoon. But sometimes that whole time is wasted and by two o'clock, all I have figured out is what happens next. And then I go on working."

Barbara Webb Robinson, now a grandmother and widowed after almost fifty years of marriage, was an only child whose father died when she was three. She and her mother, an elementary school teacher, lived with her grandparents in a small, southern Ohio River town. It was a reading family, she said. "This was Depression time and pre-television, and people read. I read, my mother read, the whole family read. On summer evenings, everyone sat on the front porch and had iced tea or lemonade. We played kick the can and caught fireflies in jars and rubbed our hand with them to make jewelry. A small town is a great place for a writer to grow up."

She began writing when she was in grade school. She did not try to sell any of her work until she had graduated from Allegheny College and was married. After five or six years of rejections, she became a successful short story writer with work published in *Ladies' Home Journal, Redbook, McCall's*, and others.

A misconception has circulated that Miss Robinson was a librarian before she became a best-selling author. "I want to correct that," she said. She was first married in "the days before women worked. You stayed home and washed and cleaned. I was in the library all the time. One day the librarian said, 'You're here all the time, would you like a job?' And I did and I had a wonderful time. But I was never a librarian."

When she is not traveling, she writes every day, "slowly but steadily," on a manual Olivetti typewriter that she ordered from the *Old Vermont Country Store* catalog. When she gets stuck, she picks up the typewriter and moves to another room. On lovely days, she pulls the shades to avoid distraction. Still, she says, working at home is difficult, especially for women: "That's where we do all the other stuff, so it's very hard to separate those two lives. Very easy, if the writing isn't going well, to say, 'I'll go put in a load of wash.' I need to resist that very strongly.

"If I'm having a tough time concentrating on the work, I'll get up in the morning, get dressed, get into the car, and go about two miles to a little breakfast place. Then come home as if I'm gong to work. That's effective. That works for me and then when it runs out, I have to do something else. It's such a funny job."

This author of children's books says that there is no greater audience than boys and girls who read: "They demand the most exciting, mysterious, touching and funniest."

She is still an avid reader. "My idea of a wonderful day would be to finish the book I'm laboring over and not have anything I have to do but sit down with a whole sofa full of books." She reads several books at a time. The one book she always takes with her wherever she goes, she told me, is *To Kill a Mockingbird*.

December Is National Stress-Free Family Holiday Month

siblings

Well, who knew? Who knew that April 10 is National Sibling Day?

My sibling probably knew it and didn't tell me. That would be just like her. Is there any stranger relationship than siblings?

Nobody makes me laugh harder than my sister. I don't laugh harder *at* anybody else than at my baby sister. For example: once she called me in tears. A client had yelled and cursed her over the phone. "You don't have sense enough to pull carrots," he screamed.

"Now, now," I told my sister, "take that for what it is. And what it is, is a lucky guess."

I don't remember if she laughed or not, but I sure did.

She gives as good as she gets. When I called her distraught about my hair, saying I looked like Albert Einstein without a big, bushy moustache, she said, "I think you could carry a big, bushy moustache."

My sister and I have a lot in common. Our parents, for one thing. Our hometown. Our March birthdays. People say we look alike and sound alike.

When I visited her last year in Tucson, her friends arriving at a party greeted me one after another with "Your hair is curly!" I thought it must be some sort of regional custom, just as people in Botswana say "Did you sleep well?" when they meet.

But I was wrong. Her friends thought I *was* my sister and that she had curled her hair for the party.

We are different, too, in many ways. After the death of our mother, my sister and I got into such a fight in the middle of Main Street, cars had to stop while we shouted it out. It was like a flash fire, grease on a stovetop perhaps, but hotter. Our cousin (a former WAC, mind you) ran for cover. It wasn't serious. It was because my sister and I process grief differently: I become more withdrawn and she becomes more extroverted. These responses are not compatible.

When we were teenagers, we could wear the same formal dresses with different effects. I, skinny and straight, would put on a strapless dress and our father would say that I looked nice. My curvaceous baby sister would put on the same dress and he would say that she could not leave the house wearing it.

As much as we enjoy one another, visits are trying. She is allergic to my cats, but the good thing is, that keeps her visits short. She is a neatnik, and the good thing is, that keeps my visits short. She lurks around corners, waiting for me to set down a coffee cup so she can rush it to the kitchen to be washed and put away before I take my second sip.

She is up at 5 A.M. singing and busy. I am up at the crack of 10 or so, moving like motor sludge on a cold day. She doesn't drink; I sometimes like a cocktail in the evening. I like to sit down once or twice in a twelve-hour period; she is never still. She likes jazz; I like classical music. That's not the only difference in entertainment preferences. When I was planning my most recent visit, she called breathlessly.

"Would you like to go to Phoenix when you're here," she asked, "to the motorcycle show? The Tuetuls will be there, from *American Chopper.*"

"What?"

"I said, would you like to . . ."

"I know what you said. I just don't know what you're talking about."

"*American Chopper.* The TV series. About custom-made motorcycles. You don't watch it?"

"Uh. No. And no, I don't want to go."

We went shopping instead.

She lives in the desert, where they consider raging humidity to be six percent. I live in northeastern Oklahoma, where ninety percent humidity is not unusual. I made the mistake of visiting her one summer and thought I would fry like bacon. One afternoon while she was at work, I staggered to the botanical gardens nearby, found the tropical garden exhibit, and lay on a bench under the mister. I didn't care what other garden visitors thought. I could breathe at last.

Her visits to northeastern Oklahoma are fraught with fussing about tornadoes and mold and ragweed.

We both love drama and musical theatre and movies and books. We love Chinese food and Mexican food and books. And we love each other.

December 31 Is the Last Chance to Make Tax-Deductible Contributions

Bless Ye Nonprofits, Every One

I might slice through the rest of the year like Scarlett O'Hara on a mean red tear, but not in December. In December I am Melanie Wilkes, gliding along with a sugary smile and a basket over my arm for the poor.

That's because December is the last chance to make year-end contributions. Probably I would scatter my largesse among the needy nonprofits even without tax deduction benefits. Thank God and the government, I am not put to the test.

I am more familiar with the other side of nonprofits: rattling the tin cup for contributions. As employee and volunteer, I have raised money for all kinds of not-for-profit agencies: arts, animals, children, disaster, education, libraries, religion, social services.

Being a nonprofit employee is hard work. It is not easy to work for a nonprofit agency. You are usually underpaid, overworked, unappreciated, and expected to be of good cheer at all times. There is never enough money or resources or time or space or equipment or personnel to do what you're trying to do. Advice, however, is free and plentiful. In the great buffet of life, advice is mounded up like commodity cheese. It comes with pity dressed up in borrowed praise.

"You people are doing wonderful work" really means "Those who can, make profits. Those who can't, do wonderful work."

How did we get to the place of thinking of not-for-profit employees as pitiful folks who ought to walk apart, ring a bell, and warn, "Unclean, unclean"?

Until the late 1800s in the United States, it was customary for good citizens to be personally involved in charitable work.

When the titans of oil, steel, and coal emerged like golden behemoths, they created philanthropic foundations, a uniquely American institution, to put a kindly face on their great fortunes. This introduced a new concept of benevolence—foundations that gave away money. From that moment, critics say, the heart went out of charity.

To fill that sentimental void, we created another revolutionary concept—tax benefits for nonprofit organizations. The rationale was not so much generosity of nature as it was a long-held mistrust of government. The nonprofit sector was expected to provide an alternative to the governmental sector in addressing society's problems.

"Though individuals may not do the particular thing so well as officers of government," John Stuart Mill wrote in *On Liberty* in 1859, "it is desirable that it be done by them rather than by government as a means to their own mental education." Also, he continued, to strengthen their activity, exercise their judgment, and develop their knowledge of the subjects.

Alexis de Tocqueville also wrote about the distinctive American proclivity for forming associations—religious, moral, educational, entertaining. In so doing, he said, "The heart is enlarged and the human mind is developed."

In other words, our doing good was for our own good, and so we are rewarded with tax benefits.

Religious organizations had been spared taxation since the Colonial period. The philosophic roots reached back to seventeenth-century England's charitable care for the poor, aged, sick, maimed soldiers and mariners, schools, bridges, ports, highways, orphans, houses of correction, and unmarried poor maids.

When the United States income tax came into existence with the Revenue Act of 1913, Congress created tax-exempt categories that included religious and charitable organizations. Fifty years later, the Supreme Court upheld the constitutionality of income tax exemption for nonprofit organizations because they provide "socially beneficial and stabilizing influences in community life."

The government is compensated for the loss of (tax) revenue, Congress has declared, by its relief from the financial burden that would otherwise have to be met by public funds. Thus the charities that depend on gifts and bequests are "a bulwark against over-reliance on big government."

With all this lofty history, how is it that employees of nonprofits, instead of being revered for their work in the public interest, scuttle about as lowly and scorned as dung beetles? "I'm gonna show you how to run that (nonprofit) place like a business," is the volunteer refrain heard across the land.

Nonprofit professionals are often slurred as dreamy and inept, yet the nonprofit organizations I have labored with could teach the profit sector some valuable lessons. By nature and necessity, most people in nonprofit organizations are resourceful, relentless, resilient, tireless, persevering, innovative, hardworking, and dedicated to their work. They are self-motivated, energetic, enthusiastic, and creative, and they usually have a sense of humor.

When I interviewed for the job of manager of a ballet company, I recited my credentials to the committee, I showed them my portfolio of my work, I laid out a plan of action, and then I told them, "Besides that, I am wearing Pavlova perfume." They laughed and hired me.

There is a new term for nonprofit workers—social entrepreneurs. A new book on the subject, *Enterprising Nonprofitism,* sings their praises: "True social entrepreneurs are innovative and resourceful; they mix passion with businesslike discipline; they take risks but know how to manage them; they are mission-driven but market savvy; and they are intensely focused on creating sustainable social impact."

At last. Not only respect, but praise.

As historian Daniel Boorstin writes, communities existed first in the United States to care for public needs, and these were communities with famously American voluntary organizations. Government followed later.

At year's end, I salute volunteers and nonprofit employees for their standard-setting work and for allowing me with my meager contribution to feel like good, kindly Melanie Wilkes.

December Is *The Nutcracker* Season

Bluebirds in Her Fingertips

Mice are scampering across the country this month, along with toy soldiers and little angels. This might be the December weather report: Hot Chocolate, followed by Sugar Plums. December is *Nutcracker* season for ballet companies.

I spent fifteen years as general manager of Tulsa Ballet Theatre, so that means fifteen years of watching *Nutcracker* rehearsals, performances, costume fittings, scenery building, lighting designs, and tours. In addition to the thirty-plus professional dancers, performances included some three hundred children performing as rabbits, mice, angels, toy soldiers, and bakers. At the center of this maelstrom were husband and wife Artistic Directors Roman Jasinski and Moscelyne Larkin. The more theatric of the two was Miss Larkin.

She is one of the famed Oklahoma Indian Ballerinas, memorialized in an Indian ballerina statue that stands next to Tulsa's Performing Arts Center, and famous for her vivacious performances in the Ballet Russe de Monte Carlo and in her variation of the Indian *pas de quatre*, *The Four Moons*.

She had retired from performing when I first met her, but she was a force of nature as a ballet teacher. Petite but terrifying.

Once, while watching a rehearsal on stage, she called out to the corps de ballet, "Will the stupid girl get in line!" Every girl stepped forward.

We were on tour with *Nutcracker* and the curtain was about to rise. Backstage she gave the cast a last look and said to one new dancer, "Angelica, has anyone told you that you look incredibly weird?" Angelica had a hairnet pulled down on her forehead in a strange way. Angelica, saucer-eyed and pale, shook her head. Miss Larkin wheeled on the rest of the dancers and demanded, "Why didn't someone tell her she looks weird? Why didn't someone help her?"

And yet she could teach children—her babies' class, she called them—with a magic that transformed them into little disciples in pink. She taught them to sit like princesses. She taught them to hold their hands just right—"as if you have bluebirds in your fingertips."

She also has a sense of joy, a laugh of gusto, and a devilment about her. We had a stack of photographs of the original *Four Moons* ballerinas—Rosella Hightower, Marjorie Tallchief, Yvonne Choteau, and Miss Larkin—all in costume and posed on the steps of the Philbrook Museum. A few of the photographs were signed, and these were collector's items that were a moneymaker for the ballet company. They were scarce. Suddenly, we had a lot more of them signed and for sale. I have a vivid memory of Miss Larkin sitting at a table merrily autographing the photos for all four dancers. "I know how to forge their signatures," she said, busy at her task.

Oklahoma's five Indian ballerinas, including Maria Tallchief, were named Cultural Treasures at the National Museum of the American Indian's opening ceremonies in Washington, D.C., in 2004.

Miss Larkin was a great mimic and a storyteller as fascinating as Scheherezade. She can tell Ballet Russe stories for hours. She has a gift for languages and, evidently, for penmanship.

She no longer teaches, coaches, or choreographs, but she still takes ballet class three times a week. Dancing is in her bones. She has been taking ballet class for seventy-six years, ever since she was three years old.

What is remarkable about seeing her at the *barre* is the illness she overcomes to take class.

A couple of years ago, Miss Larkin was diagnosed with Alzheimer's. It is a disease she knows all too well. Her mother died of it, as did her uncle and her brother. "I'm lucky," she said. "I have new medication they did not have access to."

She talks frankly about the disease and admires others who have gone public, notably Ronald Reagan and Charlton Heston. She has special praise for Nancy Reagan's campaign for stem cell research. "Stem cell research may be the answer for the future," she said.

Known as Miss Larkin to generations of dance students and as Moussia to friends, she has always been remarkably healthy and active, despite two bouts with malignant myeloma. She had virtually no injuries in her long dance career. A couple of years ago, she cracked a heel climbing over a six-foot-tall fence, then fell and broke a wrist while tap dancing with children. Except for the beginning stages of Alzheimer's, she is still remarkably healthy, still bedecked with turquoise, still a legendary beauty; and she still flashes her brilliant smile.

Her Alzheimer's symptoms crept in slowly. She began to be forgetful. That was nothing new, she said. "I've been like that all my life. Car keys!" she said, rolling her eyes. "But then I started repeating myself, saying or doing something over and over." She could rattle off her Social Security number and recall details of her dance career, but she forgot to close car doors and did not always remember the familiar route from her home to the theatre. Once she drove the wrong way through her bank's drive-in service.

Now, her conversation often zigzags from the past to the present. Occasionally she repeats herself. Her memory skims lightly over time, like a dragonfly over water.

She was born in Miami of a Russian mother and Shawnee-Peoria father. She began studying ballet at age three in the home studio of her mother, Eva Matlagova, who subsequently moved the family to Tulsa and opened a ballet studio. "I cannot remember a time I was not dancing," Larkin said, "either at powwows or in ballet class."

At the age of fifteen, she joined the Original Ballet Russe (Russian ballet), became a protégée of Alexandria Danilova's in the Ballet Russe de Monte Carlo, and toured the world with her husband, premier danseur Roman Jasinski, before his death. It was the golden age of ballet, dance historians proclaimed. Ballet Russe ballerinas were the epitome of elegance and sophistication.

When she performed in London's Covent Garden Theatre after World War II, an English critic proclaimed her "the first ray of sunshine this war torn nation has seen." In New York, she was the prima ballerina assoluta at Radio City Music Hall during the 1950s, performing four shows a day and rehearsing between performances.

As a dancer, Miss Larkin's effervescent personality was celebrated. "Remarkable for her tiny physique, sparkling personality, and tremendous jump—the greatest for her size in the contemporary theatre," writes Olga Maynard in *The American Ballet*.

The Ballet Russe was the first dance troupe to cross the United States by bus, taking ballet class beside the road and using a barbed wire fence as a *barre*. Miss Larkin, Jasinski, Michael Maule, and Danilova toured Japan, Hawaii, and the Philippines in Sol Hurok's "Great Moments of Ballet."

Larkin's memory is vivid about that time—the gift of an aquamarine from Eva Peron's sister-in-law in Argentina, signing an autograph for the royal family in Japan, making one pair of pointe shoes last for twenty performances, and dancing *Swan Lake* when she was six months pregnant with her only child. She loves to tell how partner/husband Jasinski embraced her in the ballet's tender *pas de deux* and whispered, "We are three."

Miss Larkin is celebrated for her roles in *Scheherezade, Gaite Paris-ienne, Les Sylphides, Graduation Ball,* and *The Four Moons.*

After their son, Roman Larkin Jasinski, was born, Larkin and Jasinski took the advice of dance historian Anatole Chujoy: "Go home and teach what you know." They settled in Tulsa, assumed management of her mother's studio, and transformed it into the Tulsa School of Ballet, now called the Jasinski Academy. In 1956, with Rosalie Talbot, they founded what became Tulsa Ballet Theatre. Miss Larkin is now artistic director emerita of the ballet company. Her husband died in 1991.

Today, their son, Roman, is her primary caregiver. "A family member needs lots of patience to take care of an Alzheimer's patient," he said. "A regular, daily regime is important to her well-being, and so is exercise. I can tell a difference on the days when she does move about physically."

Literature provided for caregivers of Alzheimer patients warns them to care for themselves, as well. Get support, take personal time, and "be realistic about how much you can do and about your loved one's changing ability," one pamphlet advises. "It is emotionally draining," Roman said, "and painful to witness the downward spiral. But," he added, "Mother has always been a fighter."

For decades, Miss Larkin quoted the American Indian maxim "Dance is the breath of life made visible." "Now," she says, repeating herself deliberately, "stem cell research may be the answer for the future."

I have repeated that quotation of hers about dance for years and years. After a considerable and fruitless search to authenticate the Indian legend that I had used many times when writing and speaking about her and the ballet company, I called her.

"Moussia, where does that quote—'Dance is the breath of life made visible'—come from? What tribe? I can't find it anywhere."

"Oh," she said, probably with a dismissive air of bluebird fingertips, "I made that up."

As another fund-raising project for Tulsa Ballet Theatre, we collected recipes and published a cookbook of desserts, titled *Nutcracker Sweets*. The book includes recipes from famous dancers, such as New York City Ballet's ballet master John Taras' recipe for margarita pie and Dance Theatre of Harlem's co-director Arthur Mitchell's sweet potato pie, which was his mother's recipe. The great prima ballerina assoluta Alexandra Danilova, a close friend of the Jasinskis, agreed to provide a recipe. She would not write it out or mail it, however, so I called her in New York, and she dictated it to me in her perfumed Russian accent.

I called Moussia immediately. "Oh dear," I said. "It's not a dessert at all. It's a chicken recipe. What'll I do?"

"Print it," Moussia said. "Print it exactly as she gave it to you."

It was an example of the hierarchy of the dance world. Miss Larkin terrorized the corps de ballet, but Miss Danilova terrorized Miss Larkin.

Alexandra Danilova's Honey-Curry Chicken

1 chicken cut into pieces
¼ cup mustard
⅓ cup butter, melted
4 teaspoons curry powder
½ cup honey

Melt butter and stir in honey, mustard, and curry powder. Coat chicken pieces well. Place chicken skin side down in a large, flat baking dish or pan. Bake at 350 degrees for 45 minutes. Turn chicken and cook for 15 more minutes. Serves four.

Willa Mae Mitchell's Sweet Potato Pie

2 pounds sweet potatoes
2 cups sugar
2 eggs
¼ cup butter, melted
¼ cup milk
2 teaspoons vanilla or rum extract

2 teaspoons nutmeg
2 teaspoons cinnamon
1 (9") unbaked pie shell

Boil unpeeled potatoes until soft. The peel will slip off easily when
the potatoes are done. Mash until they are the consistency of a soft
pudding. Beat in sugar, eggs, butter, milk, vanilla, nutmeg, and cinnamon until fluffy. Pour into crust and bake at 350 degrees for one
hour or until set.

Serves six to eight.

December Is Indian Nativity

Angels in White Buckskin

I live where three American Indian nations converge. I live in a state of almost seventy Indian tribes. Oklahoma has the second-largest Indian population in the United States (395,000)—not as many as California but more than Arizona.

I live in the heart of powwow country and have several fringed shawls in case I want to join in the dances. I see cars and trucks every day with Indian nation car tags. The chief of my own tribe, the largest tribe in the United States, pushes an initiative to popularize the Cherokee language. This is about tribal identity and pride. To help us learn the language, classes are offered and the monthly tribal newspaper, *Cherokee Phoenix,* always prints a story in both English and Cherokee.

I like Indian jewelry, art, and crafts. When I met Albertina Sisulu, the legendary antiapartheid activist, in South Africa, I took her a Cherokee dream catcher. She has a dream of building an after-school shelter for South African children. I told her that dream catchers are often hung over babies' cribs so that they will sleep soundly and have sweet dreams.

I scan the newspapers in early spring for announcements of wild onion suppers at Indian churches. Now I have discovered another Indian tradition—an American Indian Nativity.

One recent Christmas season, the All Tribes Community Church in Tulsa presented "'Twas in the Moon of Wintertime." Alice Whitecloud (Cheyenne/Ponca) directed the production I saw. It included a cast of sixty people from some twenty tribes. At one breathless moment, a live hawk named Valkyrie flew over the audience.

The program began with songs from the Choctaw Language Tabernacle Choir and closed with singing by Osage tribal members of the Native American Church.

The nativity story was a cacophony of colors, textures, and sounds: the sway of fringe dresses, the brilliant fabric of women's traditional dress, the needlework of fancy shawls, the melodic tinkle of jingle dresses, the pad of moccasined feet, the rhythmic sound of gourd rattles, the rustle of feathers, quills, and leggings, the soft noise of shells and beads, the movement of eagle-feather bustles, and the slash of Indian makeup.

Baby Jesus was bound snugly in a beaded cradle board. Mary wore a purple apron and traditional Mvskoke/Cherokee dress. Joseph, a Choctaw in a bristly roach headdress with bead-and-quill chest plate, soothed the baby with a lullaby played on an Indian flute.

Instead of the biblical Three Wise Men, chiefs brought sacred gifts to the baby.

One chief brought a tribal tobacco, revered for its qualities of purification. He presented a long Indian pipe, then danced to honor the child.

The Eagle Chief brought an eagle feather and fanned the baby with the breath of God. This chief, too, danced before the baby.

The Beloved Woman brought cedar, sage, and sweetgrass for healing and cleansing.

An eagle dancer presented his dance as a gift. The meaning of this gift was far beyond a performance, since song and drum are the heartbeat of a tribe. The Eagle Dance, traditional and majestic, seems to bridge heaven and earth. This is often considered the ultimate Indian dance.

A parade of hunter-warriors and messengers in priceless regalia solemnly gave the baby prized gifts of blankets, beads, soft rabbit skin, and pelts of beaver and fox.

Medicine Woman performed a jingle dance, the tins on her dress flashing in rhythm with the sound of the drum. The nativity pageant concluded with a procession of angels—beautiful young Indian girls wearing white buckskin dresses—and, finally, a rousing Stomp Dance. Members of the conservative Yuchi had to get special permission from their tribal chief to perform this dance in public. Permission was given because no admission was charged, a rule of every Indian dance I have ever attended, and donations were to benefit the church.

None of the elaborate costumes was purchased. All were handmade by relatives, in the Indian way. The Prophetess, also known as the Wise

Woman, wore a dress of deer hides made by her great-grandmother and valued at $10,000.

The names of the performers added another layer of color: Delbert Black Eyes (Lakota), Veronicah Whitecloud (Cheyenne/Ponca), Cherokee Ridge (Mvskoke/Cherokee), Coleman American Horse (Osage/Lakota), Kelly Cries For Ribs (Ponca), and Raymond and Josh Bearpaw (Yuchi/Cherokee).

I sat beside Jack Anquoe, Sr., a revered member of the Kiowa tribe and famous for his work with powwows and as a former boxer. He wanted to know why I was taking notes during the nativity. I told him I was going to write about it. "I thought so," he said.

After the final singing and the Lord's Prayer in Indian sign language, we all went downstairs to the fellowship hall for a dinner that included fry bread and grape dumplings. I had two helpings.

'Twas in the Moon of Wintertime (Huron carol)

> 'Twas the moon of wintertime
> When all the birds had fled
> That mighty Gitchi Manitou
> Sent angel choirs instead
> Before their light the stars grew dim
> And wond'ring hunters heard the hymn:
>
> Jesus, your King, is born;
> Jesus is born!
> In excelsis gloria!
>
> Within a lodge of broken bark,
> The tender Babe was found.
> A ragged robe of rabbit skin
> Enwrapped His beauty round
> And as the hunter braves drew nigh,
> The angel song rang loud and high:
>
> Jesus, your King, is born;
> Jesus is born!
> In excelsis gloria.